MW01611222

"After utilizing toolkits from The [Art of Service], I was able to identify threats within my organization to which I was completely unaware. Using my team's knowledge as a competitive advantage, we now have superior systems that save time and energy."

"As a new Chief Technology Officer, I was feeling unprepared and inadequate to be successful in my role. I ordered an IT toolkit Sunday night and was prepared Monday morning to shed light on areas of improvement within my organization. I no longer felt overwhelmed and intimidated, I was excited to share what I had learned."

"I used the questionnaires to interview members of my team. I never knew how many insights we could produce collectively with our internal knowledge."

"I usually work until at least 8pm on weeknights. The Art of Service questionnaire saved me so much time and worry that Thursday night I attended my son's soccer game without sacrificing my professional obligations."

"After purchasing The Art of Service toolkit, I was able to identify areas where my company was not in compliance that could have put my job at risk. I looked like a hero when I proactively educated my team on the risks and presented a solid solution."

"I spent months shopping for an external consultant before realizing that The Art of Service would allow my team to consult themselves! Not only did we save time not catching a consultant up to speed, we were able to keep our company information and industry secrets confidential."

"Everyday there are new regulations and processes in my industry. The Art of Service toolkit has kept me ahead by using AI technology to constantly update the toolkits and address emerging needs."

"I customized The Art of Service toolkit to focus specifically on the concerns of my role and industry. I didn't have to waste time with a generic self-help book that wasn't tailored to my exact situation."

"Many of our competitors have asked us about our secret sauce. When I tell them it's the knowledge we have in-house, they never believe me. Little do they know The Art of Service toolkits are working behind the scenes."

"One of my friends hired a consultant who used the knowledge gained working with his company to advise their competitor. Talk about a competitive disadvantage! The Art of Service allowed us to keep our knowledge from walking out the door along with a huge portion of our budget in consulting fees."

"Honestly, I didn't know what I didn't know. Before purchasing The Art of Service, I didn't realize how many areas of my business needed to be refreshed and improved. I am so relieved The Art of Service was there to highlight our blind spots."

"Before The Art of Service, I waited eagerly for consulting company reports to come out each month. These reports kept us up to speed but provided little value because they put our competitors on the same playing field. With The Art of Service, we have uncovered unique insights to drive our business forward."

"Instead of investing extensive resources into an external consultant, we can spend more of our budget towards pursuing our company goals and objectives…while also spending a little more on corporate holiday parties."

"The risk of our competitors getting ahead has been mitigated because The Art of Service has provided us with a 360-degree view of threats within our organization before they even arise."

MicroStrategy
Complete Self-Assessment Guide

Notice of rights

You are licensed to use the Self-Assessment contents in your presentations and materials for internal use and customers without asking us - we are here to help.

All rights reserved for the book itself: this book may not be reproduced or transmitted in any form by any means, electronic, mechanical, photocopying, recording, or otherwise, without the prior written permission of the publisher.

The information in this book is distributed on an "As Is" basis without warranty. While every precaution has been taken in the preparation of the book, neither the author nor the publisher shall have any liability to any person or entity with respect to any loss or damage caused or alleged to be caused directly or indirectly by the instructions contained in this book or by the products described in it.

Trademarks

Many of the designations used by manufacturers and sellers to distinguish their products are claimed as trademarks. Where those designations appear in this book, and the publisher was aware of a trademark claim, the designations appear as requested by the owner of the trademark. All other product names and services identified throughout this book are used in editorial fashion only and for the benefit of such companies with no intention of infringement of the trademark. No such use, or the use of any trade name, is intended to convey endorsement or other affiliation with this book.

Copyright © by The Art of Service
https://theartofservice.com
support@theartofservice.com

Table of Contents

About The Art of Service

The Art of Service, Business Process Architects since 2000, is dedicated to helping stakeholders achieve excellence.

Defining, designing, creating, and implementing a process to solve a stakeholders challenge or meet an objective is the most valuable role… In EVERY group, company, organization and department.

Unless you're talking a one-time, single-use project, there should be a process. Whether that process is managed and implemented by humans, AI, or a combination of the two, it needs to be designed by someone with a complex enough perspective to ask the right questions.

Someone capable of asking the right questions and step back and say, 'What are we really trying to accomplish here? And is there a different way to look at it?'

With The Art of Service's Self-Assessments, we empower people who can do just that — whether their title is marketer, entrepreneur, manager, salesperson, consultant, Business Process Manager, executive assistant, IT Manager, CIO etc... —they are the people who rule the future. They are people who watch the process as it happens, and ask the right questions to make the process work better.

Contact us when you need any support with this Self-Assessment and any help with templates, blue-prints and examples of standard documents you might need:

https://theartofservice.com
support@theartofservice.com

Included Resources - how to access

Included with your purchase of the book is the MicroStrategy

Self-Assessment Spreadsheet Dashboard which contains all
questions and Self-Assessment areas and auto-generates
insights, graphs, and project RACI planning - all with examples
to get you started right away.

How? Simply send an email to
access@theartofservice.com
with this books' title in the subject to get the
MicroStrategy Self Assessment Tool right away.

The auto reply will guide you further, you will then receive the
following contents with New and Updated specific criteria:

- The latest quick edition of the book in PDF

- The latest complete edition of the book in PDF, which criteria
  correspond to the criteria in...

- The Self-Assessment Excel Dashboard, and...

- Example pre-filled Self-Assessment Excel Dashboard to get
  familiar with results generation

- In-depth specific Checklists covering the topic

- Project management checklists and templates to assist with
  implementation

INCLUDES LIFETIME SELF ASSESSMENT UPDATES

Every self assessment comes with Lifetime Updates and Lifetime Free Updated Books. Lifetime Updates is an industry-first feature which allows you to receive verified self assessment updates, ensuring you always have the most accurate information at your fingertips.

Get it now- you will be glad you did - do it now, before you forget.

Send an email to **access@theartofservice.com** with this books' title in the subject to get the MicroStrategy Self Assessment Tool right away.

Purpose of this Self-Assessment

This Self-Assessment has been developed to improve understanding of the requirements and elements of MicroStrategy, based on best practices and standards in business process architecture, design and quality management.

It is designed to allow for a rapid Self-Assessment to determine how closely existing management practices and procedures correspond to the elements of the Self-Assessment.

The criteria of requirements and elements of MicroStrategy have been rephrased in the format of a Self-Assessment questionnaire, with a seven-criterion scoring system, as explained in this document.

In this format, even with limited background knowledge of MicroStrategy, a manager can quickly review existing operations to determine how they measure up to the standards. This in turn can serve as the starting point of a 'gap analysis' to identify management tools or system elements that might usefully be implemented in the organization to help improve overall performance.

How to use the Self-Assessment

On the following pages are a series of questions to identify to what extent your MicroStrategy initiative is complete in comparison to the requirements set in standards.

To facilitate answering the questions, there is a space in front of each question to enter a score on a scale of '1' to '5'.

1 Strongly Disagree

2 Disagree

3 Neutral

4 Agree

5 Strongly Agree

Read the question and rate it with the following in front of mind:

'In my belief,
the answer to this question is clearly defined'.

There are two ways in which you can choose to interpret this statement;
1. how aware are you that the answer to the question is clearly defined
2. for more in-depth analysis you can choose to gather evidence and confirm the answer to the question. This obviously will take more time, most Self-Assessment users opt for the first way to interpret the question and dig deeper later on based on the outcome of the overall Self-Assessment.

A score of '1' would mean that the answer is not clear at all, where a '5' would mean the answer is crystal clear and defined. Leave emtpy when the question is not applicable or you don't want to answer it, you can skip it without affecting your score. Write your score in the space provided.

After you have responded to all the appropriate statements in each section, compute your average score for that section, using the formula provided, and round to the nearest tenth. Then transfer to the corresponding spoke in the MicroStrategy Scorecard on the second next page of the Self-Assessment.

Your completed MicroStrategy Scorecard will give you a clear presentation of which MicroStrategy areas need attention.

MicroStrategy Scorecard Example

Example of how the finalized Scorecard can look like:

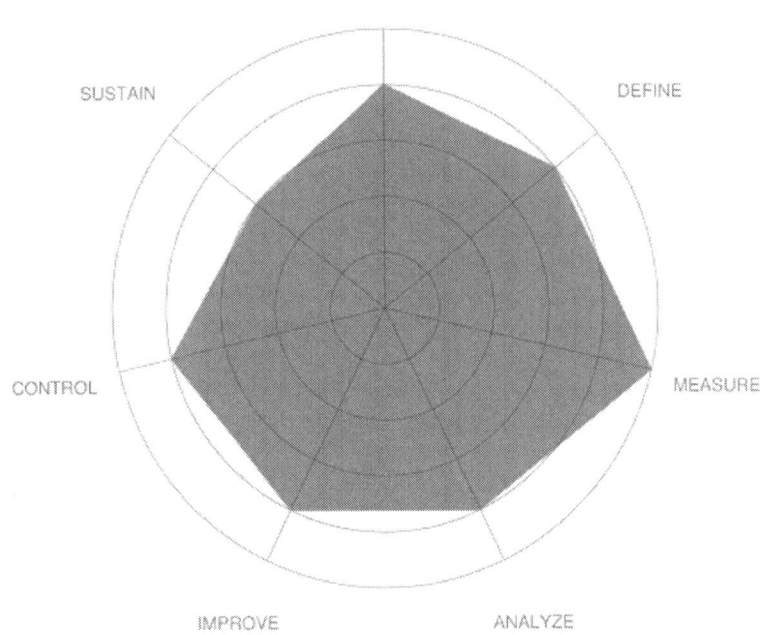

MicroStrategy Scorecard

Your Scores:

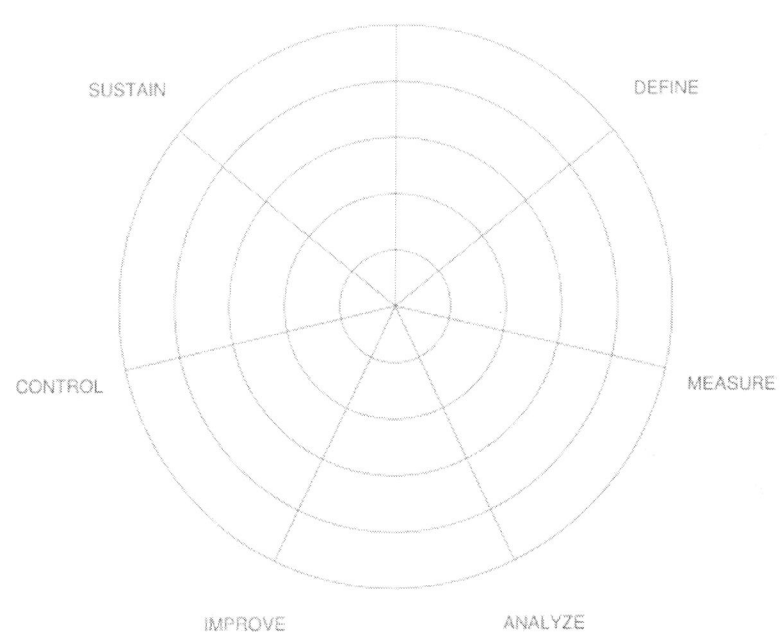

BEGINNING OF THE SELF-ASSESSMENT:

CRITERION #1: RECOGNIZE

INTENT: Be aware of the need for change. Recognize that there is an unfavorable variation, problem or symptom.

In my belief, the answer to this question is clearly defined:

5 Strongly Agree

4 Agree

3 Neutral

2 Disagree

1 Strongly Disagree

1. How are you going to measure success?
<--- Score

2. Do you need to force your web browser to prompt for a username and password?
<--- Score

3. How do you recognize an MicroStrategy objection?

<--- Score

4. What practices helps your organization to develop its capacity to recognize patterns?
<--- Score

5. Is there a problem at hand that your organization wants to tackle?
<--- Score

6. What level of detail do users need?
<--- Score

7. Do your quality management systems provide real time business intelligence that enables you to respond to quality issues rapidly?
<--- Score

8. Are losses recognized in a timely manner?
<--- Score

9. How do you recognize an objection?
<--- Score

10. How can business intelligence technology address current transportation regulation issues?
<--- Score

11. Which business areas need the most attention?
<--- Score

12. What are the expected benefits of MicroStrategy to the stakeholder?
<--- Score

13. Should you invest in industry-recognized

qualifications?

<--- Score

14. Does every organization need a CDO?

<--- Score

15. How many objects does your team need to maintain across all of your projects?

<--- Score

16. What does MicroStrategy success mean to the stakeholders?

<--- Score

17. Would you recognize a threat from the inside?

<--- Score

18. Are employees recognized for desired behaviors?

<--- Score

19. How did the skills and needs of users evolve?

<--- Score

20. How do you handle an employee that needs to be separated from your organization?

<--- Score

21. What problems have you encountered at work?

<--- Score

22. To what extent does management recognize MicroStrategy as a tool to increase the results?

<--- Score

23. Are employees recognized or rewarded for

performance that demonstrates the highest levels of integrity?

<--- Score

24. Are MicroStrategy changes recognized early enough to be approved through the regular process?

<--- Score

25. To what extent would your organization benefit from being recognized as a award recipient?

<--- Score

26. What are the key attributes, metrics and graphs that the users need to view first?

<--- Score

27. Are there recognized MicroStrategy problems?

<--- Score

28. What are the conditions that indicate a problem?

<--- Score

29. Does the issue occur all the time, or intermittently?

<--- Score

30. What is the recognized need?

<--- Score

31. How do you stay flexible and focused to recognize larger MicroStrategy results?

<--- Score

32. Are there any specific expectations or concerns about the MicroStrategy team, MicroStrategy itself?
<--- Score

33. Who else hopes to benefit from it?
<--- Score

34. How will you recognize and celebrate results?
<--- Score

35. How much are sponsors, customers, partners, stakeholders involved in MicroStrategy? In other words, what are the risks, if MicroStrategy does not deliver successfully?
<--- Score

36. What are the stakeholder objectives to be achieved with MicroStrategy?
<--- Score

37. What are the issues that you have experience in past implementations?
<--- Score

38. What problems are you facing and how do you consider MicroStrategy will circumvent those obstacles?
<--- Score

39. To what extent does each concerned units management team recognize MicroStrategy as an effective investment?
<--- Score

40. Is the need for organizational change recognized?

<--- Score

41. Are controls defined to recognize and contain problems?
<--- Score

42. As a sponsor, customer or management, how important is it to meet goals, objectives?
<--- Score

43. What situation(s) led to this MicroStrategy Self Assessment?
<--- Score

44. What specific business intelligence did your organization need from its wayside locations?
<--- Score

45. Why do you need to enter your expense allocations timely?
<--- Score

46. What will you do with your personally identifiable information?
<--- Score

47. Do you recognize MicroStrategy achievements?
<--- Score

48. When a MicroStrategy manager recognizes a problem, what options are available?
<--- Score

49. What are the minority interests and what amount of minority interests can be recognized?

<--- Score

50. How are the MicroStrategy's objectives aligned to the group's overall stakeholder strategy?
<--- Score

51. What are the important issues faced in managing MicroStrategy environment?
<--- Score

52. Will a response program recognize when a crisis occurs and provide some level of response?
<--- Score

53. What would happen if MicroStrategy weren't done?
<--- Score

54. What steps have you taken to isolate and/or resolve the issue?
<--- Score

55. Can management personnel recognize the monetary benefit of MicroStrategy?
<--- Score

56. How do you sell the idea that a greater procurement business intelligence capability is needed?
<--- Score

57. What steps have you taken to isolate and resolve the issue?
<--- Score

58. Does MicroStrategy create potential

expectations in other areas that need to be recognized and considered?

<--- Score

Add up total points for this section:

_____ = Total points for this section

Divided by: _____ (number of statements answered) = _____ Average score for this section

Transfer your score to the MicroStrategy Index at the beginning of the Self-Assessment.

CRITERION #2: DEFINE:

INTENT: Formulate the stakeholder problem. Define the problem, needs and objectives.

In my belief, the answer to this question is clearly defined:

5 Strongly Agree

4 Agree

3 Neutral

2 Disagree

1 Strongly Disagree

1. Has the improvement team collected the 'voice of the customer' (obtained feedback – qualitative and quantitative)?
<--- Score

2. What are the requirements for any new technology system in the Business intelligence space?
<--- Score

3. What are the rough order estimates on cost savings/ opportunities that MicroStrategy brings?
<--- Score

4. What are the Roles and Responsibilities for each team member and its leadership? Where is this documented?
<--- Score

5. Are stakeholder processes mapped?
<--- Score

6. Are customer(s) identified and segmented according to their different needs and requirements?
<--- Score

7. How did the MicroStrategy manager receive input to the development of a MicroStrategy improvement plan and the estimated completion dates/times of each activity?
<--- Score

8. What customer feedback methods were used to solicit their input?
<--- Score

9. What would be the goal or target for a MicroStrategy's improvement team?
<--- Score

10. How do you keep key subject matter experts in the loop?
<--- Score

11. Is there a completed, verified, and validated high-

level 'as is' (not 'should be' or 'could be') stakeholder process map?

<--- Score

12. Is MicroStrategy currently on schedule according to the plan?

<--- Score

13. If substitutes have been appointed, have they been briefed on the MicroStrategy goals and received regular communications as to the progress to date?

<--- Score

14. Is there a MicroStrategy management charter, including stakeholder case, problem and goal statements, scope, milestones, roles and responsibilities, communication plan?

<--- Score

15. How often are the team meetings?

<--- Score

16. What key stakeholder process output measure(s) does MicroStrategy leverage and how?

<--- Score

17. What are some lesser known methods to gather Business intelligence on both startups and established companies?

<--- Score

18. What is the world scope for combination of Business intelligence and cloud computing?

<--- Score

19. What specifically is the problem? Where does it

occur? When does it occur? What is its extent?
<--- Score

20. What are the compelling stakeholder reasons for embarking on MicroStrategy?
<--- Score

21. Is there a completed SIPOC representation, describing the Suppliers, Inputs, Process, Outputs, and Customers?
<--- Score

22. Is the improvement team aware of the different versions of a process: what they think it is vs. what it actually is vs. what it should be vs. what it could be?
<--- Score

23. Will team members regularly document their MicroStrategy work?
<--- Score

24. Do the problem and goal statements meet the SMART criteria (specific, measurable, attainable, relevant, and time-bound)?
<--- Score

25. What critical content must be communicated – who, what, when, where, and how?
<--- Score

26. Are improvement team members fully trained on MicroStrategy?
<--- Score

27. How is the team tracking and documenting its work?

<--- Score

28. Is the team adequately staffed with the desired cross-functionality? If not, what additional resources are available to the team?
<--- Score

29. When are meeting minutes sent out? Who is on the distribution list?
<--- Score

30. Is MicroStrategy linked to key stakeholder goals and objectives?
<--- Score

31. What are the dynamics of the communication plan?
<--- Score

32. Does the team have regular meetings?
<--- Score

33. Are you aware of the use of social networking media to obtain relevant professional and personal information when gathering competitive Business intelligence?
<--- Score

34. Will the same Portal used for Business intelligence be required to present the Legacy Applications as well?
<--- Score

35. Is the team equipped with available and reliable resources?
<--- Score

36. Is the current 'as is' process being followed? If not, what are the discrepancies?
<--- Score

37. Are there any constraints known that bear on the ability to perform MicroStrategy work? How is the team addressing them?
<--- Score

38. Is the team formed and are team leaders (Coaches and Management Leads) assigned?
<--- Score

39. How will the MicroStrategy team and the group measure complete success of MicroStrategy?
<--- Score

40. When is the estimated completion date?
<--- Score

41. How do security definitions apply to report writers, particularly proposed third-party reporting/Business intelligence software?
<--- Score

42. Are customers identified and high impact areas defined?
<--- Score

43. Are team charters developed?
<--- Score

44. Are there different segments of customers?
<--- Score

45. Who are the MicroStrategy improvement team members, including Management Leads and Coaches?
<--- Score

46. Is data collected and displayed to better understand customer(s) critical needs and requirements.
<--- Score

47. Has anyone else (internal or external to the group) attempted to solve this problem or a similar one before? If so, what knowledge can be leveraged from these previous efforts?
<--- Score

48. Is there regularly 100% attendance at the team meetings? If not, have appointed substitutes attended to preserve cross-functionality and full representation?
<--- Score

49. Is a fully trained team formed, supported, and committed to work on the MicroStrategy improvements?
<--- Score

50. Have the customer needs been translated into specific, measurable requirements? How?
<--- Score

51. How will variation in the actual durations of each activity be dealt with to ensure that the expected MicroStrategy results are met?
<--- Score

52. Are application servers required?
<--- Score

53. Is the team sponsored by a champion or stakeholder leader?
<--- Score

54. Are different versions of process maps needed to account for the different types of inputs?
<--- Score

55. Has the direction changed at all during the course of MicroStrategy? If so, when did it change and why?
<--- Score

56. Is there a critical path to deliver MicroStrategy results?
<--- Score

57. Has a high-level 'as is' process map been completed, verified and validated?
<--- Score

58. Has/have the customer(s) been identified?
<--- Score

59. Is the MicroStrategy scope manageable?
<--- Score

60. What are the boundaries of the scope? What is in bounds and what is not? What is the start point? What is the stop point?
<--- Score

61. How does the MicroStrategy manager ensure against scope creep?

<--- Score

62. Has the MicroStrategy work been fairly and/
or equitably divided and delegated among team
members who are qualified and capable to perform
the work? Has everyone contributed?
<--- Score

63. When is/was the MicroStrategy start date?
<--- Score

64. Has everyone on the team, including the team
leaders, been properly trained?
<--- Score

65. What constraints exist that might impact the
team?
<--- Score

66. How was the 'as is' process map developed,
reviewed, verified and validated?
<--- Score

67. Is full participation by members in regularly held
team meetings guaranteed?
<--- Score

**68. How do you can expand the strategy as
practice scope?**
<--- Score

69. Has a project plan, Gantt chart, or similar been
developed/completed?
<--- Score

70. Will team members perform MicroStrategy work

when assigned and in a timely fashion?
<--- Score

71. Which customers are required to activate MicroStrategy server products?
<--- Score

72. Has a team charter been developed and communicated?
<--- Score

Add up total points for this section:
_ _ _ _ _ = Total points for this section

Divided by: _ _ _ _ _ _ (number of statements answered) = _ _ _ _ _ _ Average score for this section

Transfer your score to the MicroStrategy Index at the beginning of the Self-Assessment.

CRITERION #3: MEASURE:

INTENT: Gather the correct data. Measure the current performance and evolution of the situation.

In my belief, the answer to this question is clearly defined:

5 Strongly Agree

4 Agree

3 Neutral

2 Disagree

1 Strongly Disagree

1. What is spatial or geographical analysis?
<--- Score

2. Do you have mature Business intelligence environments that can integrate fraud analytics within your current environment to take advantage of processes and architecture that are already in place?
<--- Score

3. Did you perform a ROI analysis on the project?
<--- Score

4. Is the technology sophisticated/powerful enough to sustain interactive data analysis?
<--- Score

5. Are you unable to make headway on reporting and Business intelligence projects because of an outdated chart?
<--- Score

6. Who decides based on the results of the analysis?
<--- Score

7. How important is seamless reporting and analysis to your business users?
<--- Score

8. Is data collection planned and executed?
<--- Score

9. Where will your organization increase, decrease or maintain cloud based Business intelligence / analytics investments?
<--- Score

10. What holds back a market or causes a market to decline?
<--- Score

11. What is your relation to cloud based analytics and Business intelligence applications/products currently being used within your organization?

<--- Score

12. Does the vendor provide complementary Business intelligence technologies to integrate with web analytics?
<--- Score

13. How do you anticipate embedding business intelligence and analytics within your application in the future?
<--- Score

14. What are some traits of organizations who are leaders in use of data and analytics?
<--- Score

15. Is key measure data collection planned and executed, process variation displayed and communicated and performance baselined?
<--- Score

16. Does your organization make use of Business intelligence and analytics to drive innovation?
<--- Score

17. Is data analytics/dashboards/Business intelligence integrated or is it sold in a separate module?
<--- Score

18. Do you want to take advantage of new Business intelligence (BI) and analytical capabilities?
<--- Score

19. How do business analytics and business

intelligence contribute to improve care efficiency?
<--- Score

20. Which best describes how you have embedded business intelligence and analytics within your application?
<--- Score

21. How are reports and analyses made and with which systems?
<--- Score

22. How many vendors does your organization use to supply business intelligence analytical packages?
<--- Score

23. What is your primary role in the usage and/ or management of cloud based analytics and business intelligence applications/technology within your organization?
<--- Score

24. What best practices can help enterprises reduce the total cost of ownership of Business intelligence?
<--- Score

25. Who participated in the data collection for measurements?
<--- Score

26. Is there a Performance Baseline?
<--- Score

27. How would you impact your organization?

<--- Score

28. How important is the involvement IT disciplines for new initiatives and projects in the area of business intelligence, analytics, and big data to be successful?
<--- Score

29. Why search for the cause of the crash?
<--- Score

30. What units of analysis have been used in strategy as practice research?
<--- Score

31. Have you found any 'ground fruit' or 'low-hanging fruit' for immediate remedies to the gap in performance?
<--- Score

32. Which benefits of effective business analytics/ Business intelligence does your organization currently realise?
<--- Score

33. What do customers search for when looking for Business intelligence and analytics platform suppliers?
<--- Score

34. How can analytics and Business intelligence help you perform better as your organization?
<--- Score

35. Are high impact defects defined and identified in the stakeholder process?

<--- Score

36. Where do you find information about Big Data data analysis business intelligence and etc?
<--- Score

37. How do you begin to build a better, stronger business intelligence and analytics foundation?
<--- Score

38. How much can business intelligence and business analytics help companies refine the business strategy?
<--- Score

39. Why is a mobile strategy important for effective analytics?
<--- Score

40. Does the vendor possess complementary Business intelligence technologies to integrate with web analytics?
<--- Score

41. Will closing cause you unwanted media attention?
<--- Score

42. Why has information visualization become a centerpiece in Business intelligence and analytics?
<--- Score

43. How would you rate your business maturity in the area of business intelligence and analytics?
<--- Score

44. Which benefits of effective business analytics/ Business intelligence does your organization currently realize?

<--- Score

45. Is a solid data collection plan established that includes measurement systems analysis?

<--- Score

46. Does your organization spend more time compiling data for monthly reporting than analyzing the results?

<--- Score

47. How can analytics help you optimize your organizations Business intelligence and reporting needs?

<--- Score

48. What are some of best use cases for AI when it comes to your organization data and analytics?

<--- Score

49. How much do you trust in the data quality and results analysis of your organizations business intelligence applications?

<--- Score

50. What do you have to lose, apart from poor performance and high costs?

<--- Score

51. What are the key input variables? What are the key process variables? What are the key output variables?

<--- Score

52. How much can Business intelligence and business analytics help companies refine business strategy?

<--- Score

53. What are the hardware and software requirements for MicroStrategy Analytics Express?

<--- Score

54. What causes the condition to occur?

<--- Score

55. Is your analysis already available, or do you need to begin from scratch?

<--- Score

56. Does your organization own licenses for one or more business intelligence and/or analytic tools that it wants to leverage?

<--- Score

57. Why is agile analytics so popular?

<--- Score

58. What percentage of the applications total user base uses Business intelligence and analytics on a regular basis– today?

<--- Score

59. Does your organization have a dedicated Business intelligence or Analytics office or staff?

<--- Score

60. How can the advances across the domain of analytics be effectively combined with Business intelligence methodologies to gain actionable

insights?
<--- Score

61. How large is the gap between current performance and the customer-specified (goal) performance?
<--- Score

62. Can reports provide Business intelligence style analysis on inputs and output of your automated processes?
<--- Score

63. What could data and analytics do for sales in the next decade?
<--- Score

64. Has the focus in the Budgeting Process changed since you introduced Business intelligence in your organization?
<--- Score

65. How important is it to invest in your data and analytics foundation or platform now?
<--- Score

66. Should data be replicated in the in memory engine of the analytics and BI platform?
<--- Score

67. What could data and analytics do for marketing in the next decade?
<--- Score

68. How do business analytics and business intelligence contribute to improving care

efficiency?
<--- Score

69. What are the agreed upon definitions of the high impact areas, defect(s), unit(s), and opportunities that will figure into the process capability metrics?
<--- Score

70. How effective is the current approach to end user data preparation for Business intelligence/ user analysis today?
<--- Score

71. What is the governance model for self service cloud analytics?
<--- Score

72. How is self service analytics taking Business intelligence capabilities to the next level?
<--- Score

73. What charts has the team used to display the components of variation in the process?
<--- Score

74. Are you using reporting and analysis services data warehouse and Business intelligence?
<--- Score

75. How do you use analytics to make your current enterprise business intelligence and reporting more relevant?
<--- Score

76. How do you gain access to the Quality Chart Review?

<--- Score

77. Do you currently offer embedded business intelligence and analytics as part of your application?
<--- Score

78. What is your objective for embedding Business intelligence (analytical) capabilities within other applications?
<--- Score

79. What has the team done to assure the stability and accuracy of the measurement process?
<--- Score

80. Is long term and short term variability accounted for?
<--- Score

81. Which reports and analyses are used in the different steps of the management process?
<--- Score

82. How do you increase user scalability in a distributed analytics environment?
<--- Score

83. What is the breakdown of costs by vendors, and what are the associated trends?
<--- Score

84. How do your customers view the importance of business intelligence and analytics within your application?
<--- Score

85. Who uses computerized decision support including analytics and business intelligence systems?

<--- Score

86. How does the MicroStrategy analytics engine optimize dossier performance?

<--- Score

87. Does the app integrate with your existing analytics or business intelligence platform?

<--- Score

88. What could cause more severe dislocation?

<--- Score

89. What kind of analytics do most organizations utilize when using business intelligence?

<--- Score

90. What could data and analytics do for customer service in the next decade?

<--- Score

91. How well do IT tools and resources support Business intelligence and analytics at present?

<--- Score

92. Is data collected on key measures that were identified?

<--- Score

93. How is self-service analytics taking business intelligence capabilities to the next level?

<--- Score

94. Are key measures identified and agreed upon?
<--- Score

95. What key measures identified indicate the performance of the stakeholder process?
<--- Score

96. Should data be replicated into the in memory engine of the analytics and BI tool?
<--- Score

97. What is the impact of customer longevity on customer retention and attrition?
<--- Score

98. How are the charts selected for the quality chart reviews?
<--- Score

99. Should the collection focus be on financial data?
<--- Score

100. Is Process Variation Displayed/Communicated?
<--- Score

101. Was a data collection plan established?
<--- Score

102. Do models apply to developing a data analytics system?
<--- Score

103. How can data analytic solutions help organizations?

<--- Score

104. Why geospatial analysis is important?
<--- Score

105. Why and what does behavior make difference in pattern analysis and business intelligence?
<--- Score

106. What are the advantages of using a data warehouse to analyze data for Business intelligence?
<--- Score

107. What are the most critical challenges your organization faces when orchestrating your overall business intelligence/analytics application strategy?
<--- Score

108. What is the most effective tool for Statistical Analysis Business Analytics and Business intelligence?
<--- Score

109. Why has information visualization become a centerpiece in the Business intelligence and analytics business?
<--- Score

110. How long did it take you to add business intelligence and analytics to your application?
<--- Score

111. How did the system provide cost reduction savings?

<--- Score

112. What data was collected (past, present, future/ongoing)?
<--- Score

113. Are process variation components displayed/communicated using suitable charts, graphs, plots?
<--- Score

114. How do you measure customer satisfaction?
<--- Score

115. What should a Chief Data Officers primary focus be?
<--- Score

116. What types of business intelligence and analytics capabilities do you offer within your application?
<--- Score

117. What particular quality tools did the team find helpful in establishing measurements?
<--- Score

118. Does the acquisition have multiple, existing data warehouses and Business intelligence tools to analyze information?
<--- Score

Add up total points for this section:
_ _ _ _ _ = Total points for this section

Divided by: _ _ _ _ _ _ (number of statements answered) = _ _ _ _ _

Average score for this section

Transfer your score to the MicroStrategy
Index at the beginning of the Self-
Assessment.

CRITERION #4: ANALYZE:

INTENT: Analyze causes, assumptions and hypotheses.

In my belief, the answer to this question is clearly defined:

5 Strongly Agree

4 Agree

3 Neutral

2 Disagree

1 Strongly Disagree

1. How will you leverage social media and Business intelligence to spot trends that present new customer opportunities?
<--- Score

2. Do you have the need to create snapshots for data backup, application recovery, Business intelligence, and to expedite development and testing?
<--- Score

3. How do you extract intelligence from textual data?

<--- Score

4. What channels, networks or resources are you evaluating or using to advance your business development process?

<--- Score

5. What do data driven business models look like?

<--- Score

6. What is the role of data quality in compliance, corporate performance management, Business intelligence and other critical business initiatives?

<--- Score

7. How can the customer use the profitability data during vendor negotiations?

<--- Score

8. What is the advantage of using hyper threading for a dual processor?

<--- Score

9. How can qualitative participatory crowdsourcing data be used for business intelligence?

<--- Score

10. Are you currently looking at other job opportunities?

<--- Score

11. How important is for the hiring process?

<--- Score

12. Why is data as a service so hard?
<--- Score

13. What tangible results have AI-based business intelligence applications driven in finance?
<--- Score

14. When it comes to the earnings process, what is the difference between revenues and gains?
<--- Score

15. How will business intelligence and data warehousing vendors react to market challenges, and which will lead the markets?
<--- Score

16. Do you create custom boundaries from MicroStrategy Data?
<--- Score

17. Can the enterprise manager data load run?
<--- Score

18. How will the maintenance renewal process change as a result of the conversion?
<--- Score

19. How do you Achieve the Data SLA?
<--- Score

20. How to forecast future sales based on existing sales data?
<--- Score

21. Who is responsible for and how is the support of the management process and systems arranged?

<--- Score

22. What reporting/business intelligence tool is being used for the existing your organization data warehouse?

<--- Score

23. How do you see unstructured data fitting in with your Business intelligence initiatives?

<--- Score

24. How does a MicroStrategy Desktop user access the metadata?

<--- Score

25. What will generating reports based on data from different systems imply?

<--- Score

26. How is the in memory data model managed?

<--- Score

27. Are there data warehousing or business intelligence applications that would benefit from lower latency data synchronization?

<--- Score

28. What link is there between Business intelligence and the Budgeting Process in the context of the ongoing budget debate?

<--- Score

29. What is the scope of your data quality

initiative?

<--- Score

30. What is the current business process?

<--- Score

31. How does the introduction of real time business intelligence affect the decisionmaking processes?

<--- Score

32. What risks do you see in the Business intelligence implementation as regards the Budgeting Process?

<--- Score

33. Do you have the Business intelligence you need to make the best data-driven decisions?

<--- Score

34. What are the revised rough estimates of the financial savings/opportunity for MicroStrategy improvements?

<--- Score

35. How will moving to the Cloud affect your Data Warehouse and Business intelligence platforms?

<--- Score

36. What is the best way for executives to consume all of the data needed to manage businesses?

<--- Score

37. How much data can each user import?

<--- Score

38. Is there any preferred data population, Business intelligence, or metadata management tools?

<--- Score

39. Which intelligence systems are used to support the management process and collaboration?

<--- Score

40. How are data models used in practice?

<--- Score

41. What were the financial benefits resulting from any 'ground fruit or low-hanging fruit' (quick fixes)?

<--- Score

42. Can the vendor provide proof that it can support very large databases?

<--- Score

43. Are there any parameters as regards the Budgeting Process that are particularly interesting and which have been affected by Business intelligence?

<--- Score

44. Does big data spell the end of business intelligence as you know it?

<--- Score

45. What types of partnerships, opportunities or introductions would most benefit your organization?

<--- Score

46. What tools were used to narrow the list of possible

causes?
<--- Score

47. What do next steps look like for opportunities?
<--- Score

48. How can data warehouse/business intelligence best be set up to facilitate information flows?
<--- Score

49. Is the vision data warehouse and Business intelligence reporting component a real time interface?
<--- Score

50. Which distribution centers process the most orders?
<--- Score

51. Which business initiatives does your data quality initiative support?
<--- Score

52. Is data audited on a frequent basis?
<--- Score

53. How long does the data load take?
<--- Score

54. Have you ever given any thought to modernizing your data management infrastructure to address Big Data, or improving business intelligence?
<--- Score

55. Do you want everybody to have access to all of

your data?
<--- Score

56. How efficiently and effectively can business users perform various data transformation tasks?
<--- Score

57. What about data privacy and security?
<--- Score

58. Do objects exist in the MicroStrategy metadata which match what users want to see on reports?
<--- Score

59. How will licensing, packaging and pricing models for business intelligence and data warehousing adapt to changing market needs?
<--- Score

60. What input and output measures usually are applicable to the proportional performance method for long term service contracts?
<--- Score

61. How do you plot non location based data?
<--- Score

62. How to develop best practices and stakeholder-relevant processes for Business intelligence?
<--- Score

63. What is the relationship between data, information, business intelligence, and knowledge?
<--- Score

64. Who determines the transformation rules that determine the look of Business intelligence data?

<--- Score

65. How to access change journaling data?

<--- Score

66. Does it seem like users are struggling to access data due to network bandwidth limitations?

<--- Score

67. What is the status of your organizations data governance initiative?

<--- Score

68. How do you enable self service Business intelligence without compromising on data accuracy?

<--- Score

69. How do you discover, understand, and evaluate data sources as inputs to your Business intelligence applications?

<--- Score

70. How much does a particular store, employee or process contribute to sales or profit?

<--- Score

71. Is it possible to see the data in dataset?

<--- Score

72. How can understanding the human side of data lead to innovation and effective change?

<--- Score

73. Were there any improvement opportunities identified from the process analysis?
<--- Score

74. What are the implications of globalization a data warehouse?
<--- Score

75. What does the management process look like for the entire organization?
<--- Score

76. What did the team gain from developing a sub-process map?
<--- Score

77. What tools were used to generate the list of possible causes?
<--- Score

78. Who is responsible for data quality in your organization?
<--- Score

79. How do you scale powerful data discovery applications to thousands of users while maintaining enterprise grade levels of performance, reliability, and security?
<--- Score

80. How will business intelligence and data warehousing vendors react to market challenges, and which will lead?
<--- Score

81. What key capabilities of data resource management are needed to support a useful Business intelligence system?

<--- Score

82. Does your organization gather the data that users want to see reports on?

<--- Score

83. What changes occurred in business process?

<--- Score

84. Do you have a background in data warehousing, Business intelligence or relational databases?

<--- Score

85. How much does the data compress as it is aggregated to various levels?

<--- Score

86. Is there a need to gather data from multiple sources?

<--- Score

87. What quality tools were used to get through the analyze phase?

<--- Score

88. What does the data say about the performance of the stakeholder process?

<--- Score

89. What data sources does MicroStrategy Desktop support?

<--- Score

90. Are records on the system retrieved by one or more PII data elements?

<--- Score

91. Can it be derived from the source data?

<--- Score

92. Do you increase your data storage limit?

<--- Score

93. What does your organization accomplish if you leverage the collective power of process management, technology and business intelligence?

<--- Score

94. Does the tool deliver consistently fast performance as more users and data are added to the system?

<--- Score

95. What actions/decisions are taken with the data?

<--- Score

96. What conclusions were drawn from the team's data collection and analysis? How did the team reach these conclusions?

<--- Score

97. Does all the information required exist in the existing source data?

<--- Score

98. What is the role of data integration for

enterprise data warehousing?

<--- Score

99. What criteria should be used in evaluating business intelligence and data warehouse technologies?

<--- Score

100. What are the positive effects of business intelligence for the decision making process?

<--- Score

101. Do you still need to enrich your master data in your Business intelligence application in order to satisfy your reporting needs?

<--- Score

102. Do you use or intend to use big data technology/architecture within your organization?

<--- Score

103. Were any designed experiments used to generate additional insight into the data analysis?

<--- Score

104. Does the system store data that can be used for Business intelligence as reports related to customer segmentation, orders, inventory, providers?

<--- Score

105. Is your data safe with cloud computing?

<--- Score

106. What is active data warehousing?

<--- Score

107. What can prevent a data load from working properly?

<--- Score

108. What is done with the data provided?

<--- Score

109. What is the disadvantage of using hyper threading for a dual processor?

<--- Score

110. What are the customer service industrys best practices and processes?

<--- Score

111. What is the relationship of data freshness to business value?

<--- Score

112. Are you considering modernizing your data management infrastructure or implementing business intelligence processes?

<--- Score

113. Which software solutions does your data quality initiative support?

<--- Score

114. How do you help other key players in your organization understand the importance of data and business intelligence?

<--- Score

115. How much more efficiency can be squeezed out of the manufacturing process through

traditional methods?

<--- Score

116. How do you enhance the level of end user confidence in the data warehouse?

<--- Score

117. What is the cost of poor quality as supported by the team's analysis?

<--- Score

118. How can organizations make better use of Big Data on mobile devices?

<--- Score

119. Which is a logical collection of data gathered from many databases and used to create business intelligence?

<--- Score

120. How important is being data driven to digital transformation?

<--- Score

121. How does any organization go about the process of creating the context for growth?

<--- Score

122. What does your organizations typical data warehouse and Business intelligence organizational structure look like?

<--- Score

123. Has the data been consistently captured over the time frame required for output?

<--- Score

124. How current does the data need to be?
<--- Score

125. Are you able to use your business intelligence tools to data mine the AIOps repository?
<--- Score

126. What percentage of the time do BI users view data graphically versus textually?
<--- Score

127. What were the crucial 'moments of truth' on the process map?
<--- Score

128. Do direct updates to the data warehouse mess up the Enterprise Architecture?
<--- Score

129. How does microstrategy cloud express connect to your on premise database?
<--- Score

130. What tangible results have AI based business intelligence applications driven in finance?
<--- Score

131. Has the involvement to the Budgeting Process changed since you implemented Business intelligence in your organization?
<--- Score

132. How is your organization defining the path for collecting, storing, enriching, and transforming data from disparate sources into real time business

intelligence?
<--- Score

133. Are data extraction requests for Business intelligence tools being scheduled appropriately?
<--- Score

134. Were Pareto charts (or similar) used to portray the 'heavy hitters' (or key sources of variation)?
<--- Score

135. How does your organization identify opportunities and threats in a systematic way?
<--- Score

136. What do you see the leading companies doing well when it comes to using data for digital transformation?
<--- Score

137. Which systems/algorithms/solutions to get the Business intelligence out the collected data?
<--- Score

138. What does an effective onboarding process really look like?
<--- Score

Add up total points for this section:
_ _ _ _ _ = Total points for this section

Divided by: _ _ _ _ _ _ (number of statements answered) = _ _ _ _ _ _
Average score for this section

Transfer your score to the MicroStrategy

Index at the beginning of the Self-Assessment.

CRITERION #5: IMPROVE:

INTENT: Develop a practical solution. Innovate, establish and test the solution and to measure the results.

In my belief, the answer to this question is clearly defined:

5 Strongly Agree

4 Agree

3 Neutral

2 Disagree

1 Strongly Disagree

1. How do you improve delivery management?
<--- Score

2. How will the team or the process owner(s) monitor the implementation plan to see that it is working as intended?
<--- Score

3. How is Business intelligence used in your

operational excellence initiative to improve operational efficiency?

<--- Score

4. Why would you expect positive excess returns from a risk arbitrage strategy?

<--- Score

5. Are the best solutions selected?

<--- Score

6. How to optimize a report in MicroStrategy environment?

<--- Score

7. How well does your organization develop and leverage business partnerships and strategic alliances?

<--- Score

8. What communications are necessary to support the implementation of the solution?

<--- Score

9. What business objectives are most important for your organization to address with Business intelligence solutions?

<--- Score

10. How will the group know that the solution worked?

<--- Score

11. What were the underlying assumptions on the cost-benefit analysis?

<--- Score

12. Are possible solutions generated and tested?
<--- Score

13. What is a dashboard style document?
<--- Score

14. What criteria will be used to evaluate your performance?
<--- Score

15. Does your solution provide capability to integrate with Business intelligence solutions?
<--- Score

16. Why is it important to empower business users to own and manage cpm solutions?
<--- Score

17. Are there certain scenarios/developments your organization is specifically interested in?
<--- Score

18. Is the optimal solution selected based on testing and analysis?
<--- Score

19. What is the estimated total number of users of the new Business intelligence solution?
<--- Score

20. Do decision makers adapt to time constraints?
<--- Score

21. Does your business intelligence solution require weeks or months to deploy or change?

<--- Score

22. Can traditional Business intelligence solutions – which can take months or years to deploy, and weeks or months to change – be relevant for business users today?
<--- Score

23. Who develops the dashboard screens?
<--- Score

24. How can researchers turn insights into actionable solutions?
<--- Score

25. How did the team generate the list of possible solutions?
<--- Score

26. Is pilot data collected and analyzed?
<--- Score

27. How much would you expect to spend on your organization Intelligence solution?
<--- Score

28. What tools were used to evaluate the potential solutions?
<--- Score

29. What tools were used to tap into the creativity and encourage 'outside the box' thinking?
<--- Score

30. Which bi solutions does your organization currently use?

<--- Score

31. Are improved process ('should be') maps modified based on pilot data and analysis?
<--- Score

32. How to use business intelligence to improve job profits what does project close out entail?
<--- Score

33. Is there an issue if the solution involves integration of commercial applications as MicroStrategy or a report generator, with independent licenses?
<--- Score

34. How does business intelligence solutions can streamline and influence transport networks?
<--- Score

35. What error proofing will be done to address some of the discrepancies observed in the 'as is' process?
<--- Score

36. What is your organizations appetite for risk?
<--- Score

37. What are your organizations current goals for implementing business intelligence solutions?
<--- Score

38. Do you have any suggestions for how the Business intelligence service could be improved?
<--- Score

39. What is the implementation plan?

<--- Score

40. Is a solution implementation plan established, including schedule/work breakdown structure, resources, risk management plan, cost/budget, and control plan?
<--- Score

41. Does the vendor offer a full-range of services to help you optimize your use of Business intelligence?
<--- Score

42. Are you involved in the acquisition of either business intelligence or performance management tools/solutions for your organization?
<--- Score

43. Is the implementation plan designed?
<--- Score

44. How much would you expect to pay for a BI solution?
<--- Score

45. Is there a small-scale pilot for proposed improvement(s)? What conclusions were drawn from the outcomes of a pilot?
<--- Score

46. Do report and document designers have privileges for new features?
<--- Score

47. What is the manipulation of information to create business intelligence in support of strategic

decision making?
<--- Score

48. What is how decisions are made after the implementation of business intelligence system?
<--- Score

49. How can we, in fact, realize the development approach?
<--- Score

50. How do you improve your application performance?
<--- Score

51. Is a contingency plan established?
<--- Score

52. Are new and improved process ('should be') maps developed?
<--- Score

53. What types of Business intelligence projects are more suited to distributed development?
<--- Score

54. How can Business intelligence technologies be integrated with decision support systems?
<--- Score

55. What does the 'should be' process map/design look like?
<--- Score

56. Describe the design of the pilot and what tests were conducted, if any?

<--- Score

57. What attendant changes will need to be made to ensure that the solution is successful?
<--- Score

58. Are there any constraints (technical, political, cultural, or otherwise) that would inhibit certain solutions?
<--- Score

59. How do you improve end user experience?
<--- Score

60. Were any criteria developed to assist the team in testing and evaluating potential solutions?
<--- Score

61. Has there been a management level decision to make business intelligence a priority in your organization?
<--- Score

62. Is there a master document listing all KPIs used within your organization?
<--- Score

63. How does the solution remove the key sources of issues discovered in the analyze phase?
<--- Score

64. What are the roles & responsibilities of MicroStrategy developer?
<--- Score

65. Is there a cost/benefit analysis of optimal

solution(s)?

<--- Score

**66. Who is the primary sponsor for your BI solution
for SAP?**

<--- Score

**67. How many it staff provides a supportive role
for BI solutions?**

<--- Score

**68. What unique features differentiate your
Business intelligence solution from competitive
offerings?**

<--- Score

**69. Does your organization currently use any
Business intelligence solutions?**

<--- Score

70. Was a pilot designed for the proposed solution(s)?

<--- Score

71. What is the team's contingency plan for potential
problems occurring in implementation?

<--- Score

**72. What was the primary reason for your
organizations implementation of a BI solution for
SAP?**

<--- Score

**73. Has overall corporate performance improved
in step with Business intelligence initiatives?**

<--- Score

74. What is MicroStrategy's impact on utilizing the best solution(s)?
<--- Score

75. What is Business intelligence, what does it consist of and what can be achieved by improving Business intelligence?
<--- Score

76. Will you improve customer satisfaction?
<--- Score

77. What lessons, if any, from a pilot were incorporated into the design of the full-scale solution?
<--- Score

78. What tools were most useful during the improve phase?
<--- Score

Add up total points for this section:
_ _ _ _ _ = Total points for this section

Divided by: _ _ _ _ _ _ (number of statements answered) = _ _ _ _ _ _
Average score for this section

Transfer your score to the MicroStrategy Index at the beginning of the Self-Assessment.

CRITERION #6: CONTROL:

INTENT: Implement the practical solution. Maintain the performance and correct possible complications.

In my belief, the answer to this question is clearly defined:

5 Strongly Agree

4 Agree

3 Neutral

2 Disagree

1 Strongly Disagree

1. Which application systems are users currently implementing, or are planning to implement, natively on mobile devices or remotely via the Web?
<--- Score

2. Is there a standardized process?
<--- Score

3. What quality tools were useful in the control phase?
<--- Score

4. What is the MicroStrategy Learning Portal?
<--- Score

5. Does the product have standards based hooks for integrating data with data from other business systems for data warehousing, Business intelligence, and reporting?
<--- Score

6. How do people in your organization take advantage of insights learned from business intelligence solutions?
<--- Score

7. What is a good way to plan a good career path in Business intelligence from a Reporting background?
<--- Score

8. What is the standard deviation of customer spending in each customer region?
<--- Score

9. How will the process owner and team be able to hold the gains?
<--- Score

10. Has the improved process and its steps been standardized?
<--- Score

11. Is knowledge gained on process shared and institutionalized?

<--- Score

12. How might the group capture best practices and lessons learned so as to leverage improvements?
<--- Score

13. What is the recommended frequency of auditing?
<--- Score

14. Are there documented procedures?
<--- Score

15. Is new knowledge gained imbedded in the response plan?
<--- Score

16. Does the response plan contain a definite closed loop continual improvement scheme (e.g., plan-do-check-act)?
<--- Score

17. Will the plan have separate or joint business operations units for some or all processes?
<--- Score

18. How will new or emerging customer needs/requirements be checked/communicated to orient the process toward meeting the new specifications and continually reducing variation?
<--- Score

19. Is there a transfer of ownership and knowledge to process owner and process team tasked with the responsibilities.
<--- Score

20. What other areas of the group might benefit from the MicroStrategy team's improvements, knowledge, and learning?
<--- Score

21. What information can be monitored on the website?
<--- Score

22. Is reporting being used or needed?
<--- Score

23. Will any special training be provided for results interpretation?
<--- Score

24. Are suggested corrective/restorative actions indicated on the response plan for known causes to problems that might surface?
<--- Score

25. Is there a documented and implemented monitoring plan?
<--- Score

26. How will input, process, and output variables be checked to detect for sub-optimal conditions?
<--- Score

27. Are operating procedures consistent?
<--- Score

28. Does the MicroStrategy performance meet the customer's requirements?
<--- Score

29. Does job training on the documented procedures need to be part of the process team's education and training?
<--- Score

30. How can Business intelligence facilitate organizational learning for internationalization?
<--- Score

31. What should the next improvement project be that is related to MicroStrategy?
<--- Score

32. Are documented procedures clear and easy to follow for the operators?
<--- Score

33. Have new or revised work instructions resulted?
<--- Score

34. How will the process owner verify improvement in present and future sigma levels, process capabilities?
<--- Score

35. What other systems, operations, processes, and infrastructures (hiring practices, staffing, training, incentives/rewards, metrics/dashboards/scorecards, etc.) need updates, additions, changes, or deletions in order to facilitate knowledge transfer and improvements?
<--- Score

36. What is the control/monitoring plan?
<--- Score

37. Will the strategy implementation be monitored

properly?
<--- Score

38. Does a troubleshooting guide exist or is it needed?
<--- Score

39. Who is the MicroStrategy process owner?
<--- Score

40. How will the day-to-day responsibilities for monitoring and continual improvement be transferred from the improvement team to the process owner?
<--- Score

41. Where are you in the adoption of AI and/or machine learning in your Business intelligence tools?
<--- Score

42. What can machine learning, and more specifically, deep learning, do for Business intelligence?
<--- Score

43. Is there a control plan in place for sustaining improvements (short and long-term)?
<--- Score

44. Does your wms go beyond standard reporting to offer Business intelligence and enhanced decision-making tools?
<--- Score

45. How do you plan to utilize your organizations data warehouse business intelligence system?

<--- Score

46. Are new process steps, standards, and documentation ingrained into normal operations?
<--- Score

47. How will report readings be checked to effectively monitor performance?
<--- Score

48. Is there documentation that will support the successful operation of the improvement?
<--- Score

49. Why should there be a standard process?
<--- Score

50. Is there a recommended audit plan for routine surveillance inspections of MicroStrategy's gains?
<--- Score

51. Is an sap business objects solution on your go forward plan or are you still deciding?
<--- Score

52. What are the critical parameters to watch?
<--- Score

53. What key inputs and outputs are being measured on an ongoing basis?
<--- Score

54. Is a response plan established and deployed?
<--- Score

55. Is a response plan in place for when the input,

process, or output measures indicate an 'out-of-control' condition?

<--- Score

Add up total points for this section:
_____ = Total points for this section

Divided by: _____ (number of
statements answered) = _____
Average score for this section

Transfer your score to the MicroStrategy
Index at the beginning of the Self-
Assessment.

CRITERION #7: SUSTAIN:

INTENT: Retain the benefits.

In my belief, the answer to this
question is clearly defined:

5 Strongly Agree

4 Agree

3 Neutral

2 Disagree

1 Strongly Disagree

1. Why is sales only available by primary supplier?
<--- Score

**2. Are you utilizing your Quality Assurance
Program to produce Business intelligence for use
throughout your organization?**
<--- Score

**3. What is the expectation around reporting from
the live system versus Business intelligence/
dashboards?**

<--- Score

4. How important are strategic partnerships and alliances to your business?
<--- Score

5. What was your organizations business worth?
<--- Score

6. Is it needed?
<--- Score

7. How does your organization determine who it is and where it is and how it got there?
<--- Score

8. What information is sent to MicroStrategy in the Activation XML File?
<--- Score

9. What is the most rewarding work you have ever done and why?
<--- Score

10. Which region exceeded its target?
<--- Score

11. Does server activation apply to MicroStrategy suite?
<--- Score

12. What are the critical success factors that enable self service Business intelligence success?
<--- Score

13. Are new objects available on all nodes?

<--- Score

14. What is the business meaning of the available objects?
<--- Score

15. What are the performance and scale of the MicroStrategy tools?
<--- Score

16. When is the information currently accessed?
<--- Score

17. How do you overcome the challenges of decentralized management, multiple Business intelligence systems, and fragmented implementations?
<--- Score

18. What are the MicroStrategy security risks?
<--- Score

19. What are the affordable MicroStrategy risks?
<--- Score

20. Are all users and user groups present?
<--- Score

21. How diverse is your organizations workforce?
<--- Score

22. How are sales growing for a product?
<--- Score

23. What are the common tasks associated with Business intelligence in your organization?

<--- Score

24. What are visual discovery tools?
<--- Score

25. How do you extract real business intelligence from it that will really help the business?
<--- Score

26. Why does your report display for some metric values?
<--- Score

27. Are all requirements met?
<--- Score

28. Who in your organization approved transactions?
<--- Score

29. Does the condition occur sporadically or each time a certain action is performed?
<--- Score

30. How much of the total time spent to complete a traditional Business intelligence initiative is spent on steps?
<--- Score

31. What is sales based availability and why is it important?
<--- Score

32. What systems/processes must you excel at?
<--- Score

33. What are the prerequisites to using a strategy?
<--- Score

34. How do you keep each member of the team involved and motivated?
<--- Score

35. What groups do specific users belong to?
<--- Score

36. What is your greatest weakness Regarding Junior MicroStrategy?
<--- Score

37. What is your schedule for achieving specific targets for growth?
<--- Score

38. Why are you leaving your current job?
<--- Score

39. Did you miss any major MicroStrategy issues?
<--- Score

40. Why do some legal organizations find it harder to acquire business intelligence and insights than others?
<--- Score

41. Which applications are targets for embedding Business Intelligence capabilities?
<--- Score

42. What are the best conferences to attend where there is a strong presence of Business intelligence technologies and vendors?

<--- Score

43. What knowledge or experience is required?
<--- Score

44. What are the first things you think about using business intelligence dashboard reports?
<--- Score

45. Who pays the cost?
<--- Score

46. What is static prompt in MicroStrategy?
<--- Score

47. Does server activation apply to the MicroStrategy Suite?
<--- Score

48. Which techniques have you used when designing dashboard screens?
<--- Score

49. What happens when a user loses a personal device with a corporate application installed on it?
<--- Score

50. How are MicroStrategy risks managed?
<--- Score

51. What is the value proposition for you?
<--- Score

52. What are the key business tasks supported?
<--- Score

53. What is the revenue loss attributable to customer attrition?

<--- Score

54. How satisfied to do you feel about the timeliness of your suppliers?

<--- Score

55. Is the level of communication between management, the board of directors and auditors acceptable?

<--- Score

56. What assumptions are made about the solution and approach?

<--- Score

57. Which spatial concepts may help make sense of technological, economic or other trends?

<--- Score

58. What are the MicroStrategy investment costs?

<--- Score

59. Are the differences between the mega vendors and an independent vendor like MicroStrategy significant?

<--- Score

60. What are the MicroStrategy resources needed?

<--- Score

61. How often do you currently work remotely?

<--- Score

62. What are the daily practices that materialize

strategy?
<--- Score

63. How many employees have access to the information from the business intelligence system?
<--- Score

64. How do you manage MicroStrategy risk?
<--- Score

65. How do you report a conflict of interest or potential conflict of interest?
<--- Score

66. Are the risks fully understood, reasonable and manageable?
<--- Score

67. Is target selection is totally feature based or totally indexed?
<--- Score

68. Can users and groups be added, modified, and deleted?
<--- Score

69. What is the breakdown of expenses by business units?
<--- Score

70. What reports are most commonly executed by members of a specific user group?
<--- Score

71. What is the root cause(s) of the problem?

<--- Score

72. What are the critical success factors for business intelligence systems implementation?
<--- Score

73. Does server activation apply to microstrategy reporting suite?
<--- Score

74. Which products show an increasing sales momentum?
<--- Score

75. What are your sales forecasts for next year?
<--- Score

76. Do you create, modify, and delete a prompt in MicroStrategy Web?
<--- Score

77. What are the weaknesses of your organization?
<--- Score

78. How do background checks get completed?
<--- Score

79. Where do you log into MicroStrategy?
<--- Score

80. What are the Key Performance Indicators of an effective Business Intelligence environment?
<--- Score

81. What are the clients issues and concerns?
<--- Score

82. Is your field sales force on the move or stuck in its tracks?

<--- Score

83. What happens when you export a report from Web?

<--- Score

84. Do you anticipate a convergence of content management, collaboration and Business intelligence to occur within your organization?

<--- Score

85. Are you accessing MicroStrategy from the appropriate area on your organization website?

<--- Score

86. What were the criteria for evaluating a MicroStrategy pilot?

<--- Score

87. Who should make the MicroStrategy decisions?

<--- Score

88. What gets examined?

<--- Score

89. What is microstrategy cloud platform?

<--- Score

90. Are there projects in motion for which you will inherit responsibility?

<--- Score

91. What is your biggest weakness Regarding

Junior MicroStrategy?
<--- Score

92. What are the MicroStrategy design outputs?
<--- Score

93. What are the revenue trends by business units?
<--- Score

94. What are the processes for audit reporting and management?
<--- Score

95. Are there any resources for Business intelligence stack specific patterns for the cloud?
<--- Score

96. Does subscription information already exist and how flexible is the current or future schema?
<--- Score

97. How are business intelligence tools efficient for organizational marketing operations?
<--- Score

98. Why is this needed?
<--- Score

99. Which criteria should enterprises use when selecting Business intelligence applications?
<--- Score

100. How are your organizations business intelligence tools distributed across your organization?
<--- Score

101. Is segment information useful for smaller companies?

<--- Score

102. What needs to stay?

<--- Score

103. How much time and investment does it take to deliver substantial business value with business intelligence?

<--- Score

104. Does sales information exist for each of your products?

<--- Score

105. How is information shared and how do managers collaborate?

<--- Score

106. How will you comply with your organization during emergency situations?

<--- Score

107. What is your organization culture like?

<--- Score

108. What are your departments best practices for conducting real time business intelligence?

<--- Score

109. Why is the app hanging while trying to access a door through any method?

<--- Score

110. What aspects of an AI system can be patented?
<--- Score

111. Why should business intelligence be the foundation for corporate performance management?
<--- Score

112. What can bi vendors do to become more customer centric?
<--- Score

113. Why the need?
<--- Score

114. What is your advice to an executive or manager who feels like organization is behind?
<--- Score

115. What is the problem and/or vulnerability?
<--- Score

116. Do you make an anonymous report?
<--- Score

117. Do you run time triggered subscriptions?
<--- Score

118. Do you create, modify, and delete a filter in MicroStrategy Web?
<--- Score

119. Are changes to users and groups synchronized across all nodes in the cluster?
<--- Score

120. Where is the connection information stored?
<--- Score

121. How do you build the right business case?
<--- Score

122. What technological breakthroughs will enable the emergence of the next generation of business intelligence applications?
<--- Score

123. Are performance appraisals used efficiently?
<--- Score

124. What about the argument that other organizations can put spare cash to better use by buying back own shares?
<--- Score

125. How can risk management be tied procedurally to process elements?
<--- Score

126. How should the information be incorporated the customer information service?
<--- Score

127. What types of reports do users expect?
<--- Score

128. Why would your organization endeavor to implement a strategic Business intelligence program?
<--- Score

129. Do bi vendors make considerable changes in software each year with each new upgrade?

<--- Score

130. How can more rows be included on the report?

<--- Score

131. Is the pii shared with other organizations?

<--- Score

132. Does microstrategy adhere to best practices for software activation?

<--- Score

133. What differentiates your organization from competitors?

<--- Score

134. What is your organization-of-the-art in the area of Business intelligence (BI) Technologies?

<--- Score

135. What vendors dominate the DSS product space?

<--- Score

136. How does self-service business intelligence enable organizational agility in a multi-sided platform?

<--- Score

137. What is the extent or complexity of the MicroStrategy problem?

<--- Score

138. Did microstrategy attempt to manipulate accounting numbers?
<--- Score

139. What is used to lock the server to a machine?
<--- Score

140. Do you create, modify, and delete a report in Desktop?
<--- Score

141. Is the password for the authentication user correct?
<--- Score

142. Does management have the right priorities among projects?
<--- Score

143. Do the viable solutions scale to future needs?
<--- Score

144. How did the market view the deal upon its announcement?
<--- Score

145. What does the MicroStrategy Mobile product provide?
<--- Score

146. Where do you can go to find good strategy practices?
<--- Score

147. How are inquiries allocated across distribution channels and the sales organization?

<--- Score

148. What sets microstrategy mobile apps apart?
<--- Score

149. What type of work environment do you prefer?
<--- Score

150. Does the platform generate business intelligence that predicts the behaviors of adverse parties?
<--- Score

151. How do users currently access information?
<--- Score

152. Would you develop a MicroStrategy Communication Strategy?
<--- Score

153. Does the tool possess Business intelligence (BI) capability or do you have another tool that does?
<--- Score

154. Do vendor agreements bring new compliance risk ?
<--- Score

155. What business benefit do empty set rows provide?
<--- Score

156. Should the details of each report be displayed alongside each report?

<--- Score

157. Are your microstrategy web customizations present?
<--- Score

158. What are logical views used for in MicroStrategy?
<--- Score

159. What are the requirements for audit information?
<--- Score

160. When did the condition first occur?
<--- Score

161. How will the MicroStrategy data be captured?
<--- Score

162. How much memory does intelligence server use when it starts up?
<--- Score

163. How many individuals PII is in the system?
<--- Score

164. Do kpis in use link to specific business goals?
<--- Score

165. What role does business intelligence play in publishers digital content publishing efforts?
<--- Score

166. Where is training needed?
<--- Score

167. How do you find information on the web?
<--- Score

168. Does microstrategy adhere to software activation best practices?
<--- Score

169. Does the problem have ethical dimensions?
<--- Score

170. Is the information related/structured or unrelated/unstructured?
<--- Score

171. Is the graphical interface functional enough for power users and easy enough for casual users?
<--- Score

172. What are the critical success factors that enable self-service business intelligence success?
<--- Score

173. Are compensation and benefits correctly related to titles and job descriptions?
<--- Score

174. What are the various groups that use the system?
<--- Score

175. What business objectives are you currently targeting with your business intelligence system?
<--- Score

176. What is the business you are in?

<--- Score

177. Are you running out of policy tools?

<--- Score

178. What is a good logical next step from being a program manager in Business intelligence?

<--- Score

179. Are you missing MicroStrategy opportunities?

<--- Score

180. How much data can be collected in the given timeframe?

<--- Score

181. What are the trends in revenue, by revenue types?

<--- Score

182. How will the change process be managed?

<--- Score

183. Is the work to date meeting requirements?

<--- Score

184. When should a process be art not science?

<--- Score

185. How would resources be deployed between your work sites and your offshore providers locations for a typical Business intelligence project?

<--- Score

186. Are other organizations facing new pressures

to embrace a robust Business intelligence (BI) platform?

<--- Score

187. Are procedures documented for managing MicroStrategy risks?

<--- Score

188. What is the actual amount of profit margin by business unit or region?

<--- Score

189. What is the meaning of your organization?

<--- Score

190. Who are the key business users supported?

<--- Score

191. What are the costs?

<--- Score

192. How do you view the full column?

<--- Score

193. What will your organization gain from using a geographically distributed team for your Business intelligence projects?

<--- Score

194. Where do you find your organization invoice payment information?

<--- Score

195. Do you apply social and Business intelligence innovations to work flow transformation in your legal business and as it relates to increased

customer/client interactivity?

<--- Score

196. How is strategy as practice similar and/or different to corporate strategy?

<--- Score

197. What MicroStrategy events should you attend?

<--- Score

198. When were you most satisfied in your job Regarding Junior MicroStrategy?

<--- Score

199. What is a worst-case scenario for losses?

<--- Score

200. Why do you have to provide it again to access certain applications?

<--- Score

201. Why do you use homegrown BI applications some or all of the time?

<--- Score

202. What was one difficulty you had using the software?

<--- Score

203. Are your organizations competitors restating for similar reasons?

<--- Score

204. What types of personalities do you work with best?

<--- Score

205. What qualities do you believe are important to have as a manager?
<--- Score

206. What are microstrategy mobile powered apps?
<--- Score

207. Which is your Business intelligence vendor and which Business intelligence tools do you use?
<--- Score

208. What is the nature of your organization?
<--- Score

209. What is the prompted/non prompted report mix?
<--- Score

210. How does a customer with limited technical experience choose a new business intelligence platform?
<--- Score

211. What is the best strategy for driving adoption of new reporting applications across the enterprise?
<--- Score

212. Has sox affected the relationship of smaller companies with auditing firms?
<--- Score

213. Where is the cost?

<--- Score

214. Which issues are too important to ignore?
<--- Score

215. Who are the MicroStrategy decision-makers?
<--- Score

216. Are there regulatory / compliance issues?
<--- Score

217. Is there any way to speed up the process?
<--- Score

218. What is the relationship between Business intelligence and strategic competitive advantage?
<--- Score

219. What MicroStrategy data should be managed?
<--- Score

220. What does your organization expect you to do?
<--- Score

221. What MicroStrategy coordination do you need?
<--- Score

222. What is microstrategy operations manager used for?
<--- Score

223. What is the Total Addressable Market TAM for Business Intelligence BI in your segment industry?

<--- Score

224. Are the most efficient solutions problem-specific?

<--- Score

225. What are the strengths about your organization?

<--- Score

226. How do you imagine a typical day of an employee in your organization Regarding Junior MicroStrategy?

<--- Score

227. Does your product have a six minute sales cycle or a six month sales cycle?

<--- Score

228. What does the MicroStrategy Server product provide?

<--- Score

229. What schedule do you hope to work?

<--- Score

230. How many kpis exist at each levels of your organization?

<--- Score

231. What are the strategic priorities for this year?

<--- Score

232. Is the management reasonably efficient?

<--- Score

233. Are you entering your username and password correctly?

<--- Score

234. What management, organization, and technology factors had to be addressed in providing Business intelligence capabilities for each type of user?

<--- Score

235. How do you report a suspected compliance concern?

<--- Score

236. How long to keep data and how to manage retention costs?

<--- Score

237. When asked, which ai capabilities in your Business intelligence tools are most important to you?

<--- Score

238. What are the advantages and disadvantages you experience with using Business intelligence?

<--- Score

239. How do you contact your model application Help Desk?

<--- Score

240. What happens when intelligence server starts?

<--- Score

241. How can systematic reviews incorporate

qualitative research?

<--- Score

242. Which MicroStrategy data should be retained?

<--- Score

243. How could your organization ever pay its debts?

<--- Score

244. Is one willing to take a serious interest in the business of investment?

<--- Score

245. What happens when intelligence server stops?

<--- Score

246. Which operating systems and versions are supported?

<--- Score

247. Does the condition occur on all machines or just on one?

<--- Score

248. Do you have direct access to Business intelligence (BI) systems in your current role?

<--- Score

249. Do you have an issue in getting priority?

<--- Score

250. What resources or support might you need?

<--- Score

251. Do you know anyone that works with your organization?

<--- Score

252. How do you refer to your system or project?

<--- Score

253. Is the information sent to MicroStrategy secure?

<--- Score

254. Who will facilitate the team and process?

<--- Score

255. How many kpis exist in your organization?

<--- Score

256. Who should be sent information services?

<--- Score

257. Who contacts a payer to negotiate rates for a new contract?

<--- Score

258. How much experience do you have with pulling MicroStrategy reports?

<--- Score

259. Is MicroStrategy documentation maintained?

<--- Score

260. Is there any other MicroStrategy solution?

<--- Score

261. How many content information objects and/

or subscription information objects will be used?

<--- Score

262. Which forward looking information and metrics are missing?

<--- Score

263. Are the key business and technology risks being managed?

<--- Score

264. What are the most reported benefits of the successful implementation of business intelligence?

<--- Score

265. Will your organization commit to implementation schedule?

<--- Score

266. How do you architect dashboards and scorecards?

<--- Score

267. How can you better manage risk?

<--- Score

268. Which employee benefits are the most popular, and which do you pare down?

<--- Score

269. What is the difference between Business intelligence and self-service Business intelligence?

<--- Score

270. How much of a pay cut would you take to

work remotely more often?

<--- Score

271. How do you deal with MicroStrategy risk?

<--- Score

272. How do you access information using MicroStrategy?

<--- Score

273. How would you rate the level of customer service and technical support?

<--- Score

274. What is the significance of customer acceptance provisions?

<--- Score

275. Will current investments in legacy systems be stranded?

<--- Score

276. Is there a strict change management process?

<--- Score

277. When should you expect the backlash from users and companies?

<--- Score

278. How would you rate your organizations Business intelligence and reporting capabilities?

<--- Score

279. Why do tier one financial services providers turn to microstrategy?

<--- Score

280. Can you integrate quality management and risk management?

<--- Score

281. Has sox affected the relationship of smaller companies with shareholders?

<--- Score

282. Can it be used as a means of busting information silos to create new Business intelligence – and streamline compliance too?

<--- Score

283. What did you dislike about your old job?

<--- Score

284. What are your organizations most widely held beliefs or values?

<--- Score

285. What were your key business objectives?

<--- Score

286. Will the tpa have any independent settlement authority, or will your organization retain all authority?

<--- Score

287. When should information services be sent to customers?

<--- Score

288. How do profit margins in each region compare to the same period last year?

<--- Score

289. What other Business intelligence system gives you insight into cultural values that determine the success or failure of products and services?
<--- Score

290. How do you handle types of situations?
<--- Score

291. Do ldap users have own inbox and personal folders?
<--- Score

292. How can organizations go about the implementation of effective governance programs?
<--- Score

293. Are there performance constraints or additional fees when it comes to business intelligence?
<--- Score

294. What role does AI play in delivering new insights and business intelligence from your apps?
<--- Score

295. Is social BI a separate category of business intelligence or ultimately a feature embedded into broader offerings?
<--- Score

296. What do you know about your organization?
<--- Score

297. Which needs are not included or involved?

<--- Score

298. How can business intelligence provide strategic guidance and execution support across the business?
<--- Score

299. What are the expected MicroStrategy results?
<--- Score

300. What challenges may your organization face when migrating to and running business in the cloud?
<--- Score

301. Do you align your Business intelligence content with your corporate objectives and strategies?
<--- Score

302. How does intelligence server use memory after it is running?
<--- Score

303. Who should resolve the MicroStrategy issues?
<--- Score

304. What is the MicroStrategy business impact?
<--- Score

305. How long are employees staying with your organization?
<--- Score

306. How will business intelligence software vendors react to ongoing market shifts and

challenges?
<--- Score

307. Is risk periodically assessed?
<--- Score

308. What is microstrategy server activation?
<--- Score

309. How does cpm link to Business intelligence, erp and other business applications, and how do you choose the right technology components?
<--- Score

310. What MicroStrategy data will be collected?
<--- Score

311. Are you familiar with BI concepts?
<--- Score

312. What does the MicroStrategy Web product provide?
<--- Score

313. What has changed within your organization to reduce the likelihood of a restatement happening again?
<--- Score

314. Are there any trends in the business over the past six quarters?
<--- Score

315. What are the annual revenues of your organization?
<--- Score

316. What organization department would have the authority?

<--- Score

317. Can the authentication user log in as an LDAP user?

<--- Score

318. Why are sales only available by primary supplier?

<--- Score

319. How many it staff work in your organization at your site?

<--- Score

320. Why are microstrategy business apps unique?

<--- Score

321. Which parts of the Business Intelligence architecture are most suitable for implementing Power BI?

<--- Score

322. Are customers ignoring the advice and best practices of Business intelligence vendors?

<--- Score

323. What are the generic steps thereof?

<--- Score

324. How efficient are you at completing the sales cycle?

<--- Score

325. Does the system offer multi matter,multi party and business intelligence capabilities?

<--- Score

326. Who needs budgets?

<--- Score

327. What are the critical success factors for Business intelligence system implementation?

<--- Score

328. What effect will it have on employee satisfaction?

<--- Score

329. Who are the MicroStrategy decision makers?

<--- Score

330. Which business units are hitting targets?

<--- Score

331. What is the link between tacit knowledge and its conversion to Business intelligence and action?

<--- Score

332. What are the biggest challenges your organization faces when orchestrating its business intelligence strategy?

<--- Score

333. Where should the customer information service be delivered?

<--- Score

334. Which techniques are important for embedding Business intelligence content and

functions?

<--- Score

335. Are risk management tasks balanced centrally and locally?

<--- Score

336. How to use value prompt and drag it on to report editor?

<--- Score

337. What is the median spending of customers in each customer region?

<--- Score

338. How materiality enable and constraint the strategy work?

<--- Score

339. Is there something regarding Business intelligence that you wish you could do, that you cannot in the current situation?

<--- Score

340. What implementation strategy should therefore be adopted?

<--- Score

341. Why would your organization prefer gross revenue reporting over net revenue reporting?

<--- Score

342. How to face top management with inclusive approach?

<--- Score

343. What is competitive intelligence?
<--- Score

344. What was the biggest benefit to your organization?
<--- Score

345. What do you do if a vendor requests an address or name change?
<--- Score

346. Why is microstrategy changing its product packaging?
<--- Score

347. Are MicroStrategy vulnerabilities categorized and prioritized?
<--- Score

348. What creative shifts do you need to take?
<--- Score

349. How many offices does your organization have?
<--- Score

350. Is your business located at Service Address?
<--- Score

351. What risks do you need to manage?
<--- Score

352. How many customers exist in each customer region?
<--- Score

353. How you can create the Intelligent cubes in MicroStrategy?

<--- Score

354. Are there any blackout periods while you upgrade the system?

<--- Score

355. How will it affect your organizations reputation?

<--- Score

356. Where do you need to exercise leadership?

<--- Score

357. Does the restatement reflect poorly on the integrity of management?

<--- Score

358. What is the procedure for activating Server Installations?

<--- Score

359. How would you rate the staff in timeliness?

<--- Score

360. What power relations do exist between practitioners in strategy work?

<--- Score

361. What types of data do your MicroStrategy indicators require?

<--- Score

362. Why should you use MicroStrategy?

<--- Score

363. What MicroStrategy standards are applicable?
<--- Score

364. Is the quality assurance team identified?
<--- Score

365. How is sales based availability calculated and how do you know that it is accurate?
<--- Score

366. Is there a strategy behind the success of the top performers?
<--- Score

367. Do you actually have the right culture inside your organization?
<--- Score

368. Does the microstrategy web authentication method used work?
<--- Score

369. What is a time you exercised leadership?
<--- Score

370. What types of side agreements can turn a sale into a consignment?
<--- Score

371. How many can each vendor deliver?
<--- Score

372. When will discoverer become obsolete and a migration to business intelligence necessary?
<--- Score

373. What are the weaknesses about your organization?

<--- Score

374. Which of implementations or tools you select?

<--- Score

375. What are the business benefits of the implementation of governance?

<--- Score

376. Who owns what data?

<--- Score

377. What does your organization gain by integrating Business intelligence technologies with service-oriented architectures (SOA)?

<--- Score

378. Are you looking to take your well functioning Business intelligence or information management program to the next level?

<--- Score

379. Which is your organizations industry?

<--- Score

380. Is the MicroStrategy risk managed?

<--- Score

381. Whom do you really need or want to serve?

<--- Score

382. What are the concrete MicroStrategy results?

<--- Score

383. What is MicroStrategy risk?

<--- Score

384. Do you have any other Business intelligence, ETL Tools, App Dev Tools, or other modeling tools?

<--- Score

385. Which metric represents the maximum possible value in the bullet?

<--- Score

386. What content should be included in customer information services?

<--- Score

387. What is your customer trying to achieve?

<--- Score

388. Do you have the optimal project management team structure?

<--- Score

389. What is the average spending of customers in each customer region?

<--- Score

390. How does a user connect to MicroStrategy Intelligence Server?

<--- Score

391. Is crimping a contact onto a wire a secret?

<--- Score

392. Who is involved in the management review process?

<--- Score

393. What criteria will you use to assess your MicroStrategy risks?
<--- Score

394. Why should the interactive condition be applied on the Web?
<--- Score

395. Do you have a formal partnering strategy?
<--- Score

396. How are training requirements identified?
<--- Score

397. How has the availability of information changed since you implemented Business intelligence in your organization?
<--- Score

398. How satisfied are you with your vendor and product for embedded business intelligence?
<--- Score

399. What are your sales volumes, sales trends, and top materials and customers for the year?
<--- Score

400. Who is responsible for which systems and which activities are associated?
<--- Score

401. What objects are duplicated with a project?
<--- Score

402. How long does it take to get approved for access to a requested application or role?

<--- Score

403. What happens if the system crashes or fails?

<--- Score

404. Does your organization utilize Business intelligence software to augment system reporting?

<--- Score

405. What factors are critical when considering use of distributed teams for Business intelligence projects?

<--- Score

406. What type of information might be available to you regarding business reporting or Business intelligence?

<--- Score

407. How compatible is it with your organizations capacity and culture?

<--- Score

408. What difficulties did you experience during implementation?

<--- Score

409. How do you configure anonymous access to a MicroStrategy Intelligence Server?

<--- Score

410. Why do you want to provide a new publication on Business intelligence and

dimensional modeling?

<--- Score

411. Will the system tell you when your password is about to expire?

<--- Score

412. Do you prefer written or verbal communication Regarding Junior MicroStrategy?

<--- Score

413. Are intelligence server statistics being logged correctly?

<--- Score

414. How to do performance tuning on reports?

<--- Score

415. Where do you find key metrics associated with your organization?

<--- Score

416. What people, organization, and technology factors had to be addressed in providing Business intelligence capabilities for each type of user?

<--- Score

417. What are the total sales for red items?

<--- Score

418. Are there Business intelligence tools already in place elsewhere in your organization?

<--- Score

419. How is desktop different from prior versions of MicroStrategy?

<--- Score

420. Which areas of your organization have more returns?
<--- Score

421. What is your plan to assess your security risks?
<--- Score

422. How will the data be checked for quality?
<--- Score

423. How does your organization evaluate strategic MicroStrategy success?
<--- Score

424. What is the level of cooperation with your Business intelligence/customer intelligence practice?
<--- Score

425. How would you rate your organizations Business intelligence / reporting capabilities?
<--- Score

426. Where do the MicroStrategy decisions reside?
<--- Score

427. Is the MicroStrategy solution sustainable?
<--- Score

428. What, related to, MicroStrategy processes does your organization outsource?
<--- Score

429. What is intelligence in business?
<--- Score

430. Who manages supplier risk management in your organization?
<--- Score

431. What was the most difficult employee situation you found yourself Regarding Junior MicroStrategy?
<--- Score

432. Who should you contact for MicroStrategy support?
<--- Score

433. What users will be impacted?
<--- Score

434. Who are the key stakeholders for the MicroStrategy evaluation?
<--- Score

435. Why is server activation necessary?
<--- Score

436. What kind of business did buyers get for that price?
<--- Score

437. What is the difference between business intelligence and self service business intelligence?
<--- Score

438. Is key information and Business intelligence unavailable throughout your organization?

<--- Score

439. Does microstrategy adhere to software activation common practices?
<--- Score

440. How much history is available from the operational systems?
<--- Score

441. What MicroStrategy capabilities do you need?
<--- Score

442. How important is the earlier experience of a certain field of industry before starting to work in Business intelligence?
<--- Score

443. Are events managed to resolution?
<--- Score

444. What does the MicroStrategy Architect product provide?
<--- Score

445. Has it done a good job for its shareholders?
<--- Score

446. How are sales representatives performing?
<--- Score

447. How do you view different weeks?
<--- Score

448. Is there an established change management process?

<--- Score

449. Why use microstrategy object manager?
<--- Score

450. Why has your report performance gone down?
<--- Score

451. How do you identify subcontractor relationships?
<--- Score

452. What alternative responses are available to manage risk?
<--- Score

453. Do you have organizational privacy requirements?
<--- Score

454. Are the user credentials correct?
<--- Score

455. What are the essential qualities of your organization?
<--- Score

456. How feasible is the strategy technologically and logistically?
<--- Score

457. What is the value of assets, liabilities, and owners equity on a given date?
<--- Score

458. Who has time to go through all that?
<--- Score

459. What is the primary obstacle to convergence of content management, collaboration, and Business intelligence within your organization?
<--- Score

460. How do you experience that the availability of information Business intelligence allows has affected your organization?
<--- Score

461. What is your organization turnaround time for approval?
<--- Score

462. Who needs to know?
<--- Score

463. How will corresponding data be collected?
<--- Score

464. Does the system collect, maintain, use or share PII?
<--- Score

465. Do you understand your management processes today?
<--- Score

466. How middle managers obtain more power and influence in strategy work?
<--- Score

467. Do you believe SOX has enhanced, or

diminished, the value of smaller companies?
<--- Score

468. How much experience do you have?
<--- Score

469. What do employees need in the short term?
<--- Score

470. What percentage of leads are converted into sales?
<--- Score

471. Are there skillsets missing in your organization?
<--- Score

472. Have you dealt with Business intelligence in the past or presently and if so in what capacity?
<--- Score

473. How many trainings, in total, are needed?
<--- Score

474. Are subscriptions load balanced across all servers?
<--- Score

475. What are the values of assets and liabilities on a given date?
<--- Score

476. Are you attempting to access the system while it is unavailable?
<--- Score

477. Is termination condition reached?
<--- Score

478. Do you need to do a usability evaluation?
<--- Score

Add up total points for this section:
_ _ _ _ _ = Total points for this section

Divided by: _ _ _ _ _ _ (number of
statements answered) = _ _ _ _ _ _
Average score for this section

Transfer your score to the MicroStrategy
Index at the beginning of the Self-
Assessment.

MicroStrategy and Managing Projects, Criteria for Project Managers:

1.0 Initiating Process Group: MicroStrategy

1. Did the MicroStrategy project team have the right skills?

2. Measurable - are the targets measurable?

3. How to control and approve each phase?

4. What are the tools and techniques to be used in each phase?

5. What will be the pressing issues of tomorrow?

6. Are you properly tracking the progress of the MicroStrategy project and communicating the status to stakeholders?

7. At which cmmi level are software processes documented, standardized, and integrated into a standard to-be practiced process for your organization?

8. If the risk event occurs, what will you do?

9. How will you do it?

10. When will the MicroStrategy project be done?

11. Have you evaluated the teams performance and asked for feedback?

12. Establishment of pm office?

13. During which stage of Risk planning are risks prioritized based on probability and impact?

14. Mitigate. what will you do to minimize the impact should the risk event occur?

15. Do you know the roles & responsibilities required for this MicroStrategy project?

16. When must it be done?

17. What were things that you need to improve?

18. How will you know you did it?

19. The process to Manage Stakeholders is part of which process group?

20. How well did the chosen processes fit the needs of the MicroStrategy project?

1.1 Project Charter: MicroStrategy

21. Environmental stewardship and sustainability considerations: what is the process that will be used to ensure compliance with the environmental stewardship policy?

22. Assumptions and constraints: what assumptions were made in defining the MicroStrategy project?

23. What are the assigned resources?

24. Where and how does the team fit within your organization structure?

25. Why use a MicroStrategy project charter?

26. Why is a MicroStrategy project Charter used?

27. When is a charter needed?

28. How much?

29. How high should you set your goals?

30. Who are the stakeholders?

31. Market – identify products market, including whether it is outside of the objective: what is the purpose of the program or MicroStrategy project?

32. If finished, on what date did it finish?

33. What date will the task finish?

34. Major high-level milestone targets: what events measure progress?

35. What is the business need?

36. How will you know that a change is an improvement?

37. Must Have?

38. What barriers do you predict to your success?

39. Customer: who are you doing the MicroStrategy project for?

40. How will you know a change is an improvement?

1.2 Stakeholder Register: MicroStrategy

41. How big is the gap?

42. What & Why?

43. Who is managing stakeholder engagement?

44. Who wants to talk about Security?

45. What is the power of the stakeholder?

46. How much influence do they have on the MicroStrategy project?

47. What are the major MicroStrategy project milestones requiring communications or providing communications opportunities?

48. What opportunities exist to provide communications?

49. How should employers make voices heard?

50. How will reports be created?

51. Is your organization ready for change?

1.3 Stakeholder Analysis Matrix: MicroStrategy

52. Who holds positions of responsibility in interested organizations?

53. Insurmountable weaknesses?

54. Where are the good opportunities facing your organizations development?

55. Which resources are required?

56. Benefit to whom?

57. Accreditations, qualifications, certifications?

58. Who has control over whom?

59. How affected by the problem(s)?

60. Cashflow, start-up cash-drain?

61. Business and product development?

62. What actions can be taken to reduce or mitigate risk?

63. How does the MicroStrategy project involve consultations or collaboration with other organizations?

64. Which conditions out of the control of the

management are crucial for the achievement of the immediate objective?

65. Which conditions out of the control of the management are crucial to contribute for the achievement of the development objective?

66. Are they likely to influence the success or failure of your MicroStrategy project?

67. What tools would help you communicate?

68. Why is it important to identify them?

69. What is the issue at stake?

70. How to measure the achievement of the Immediate Objective?

71. Participatory approach: how will key stakeholders participate in the MicroStrategy project?

2.0 Planning Process Group: MicroStrategy

72. How well will the chosen processes produce the expected results?

73. How will users learn how to use the deliverables?

74. Are the follow-up indicators relevant and do they meet the quality needed to measure the outputs and outcomes of the MicroStrategy project?

75. How can you tell when you are done?

76. What are the different approaches to building the WBS?

77. To what extent do the intervention objectives and strategies of the MicroStrategy project respond to your organizations plans?

78. Did you read it correctly?

79. Explanation: is what the MicroStrategy project intents to solve a hard question?

80. What type of estimation method are you using?

81. Do the partners have sufficient financial capacity to keep up the benefits produced by the programme?

82. Why do it MicroStrategy projects fail?

83. In what way has the program contributed towards the issue culture and development included on the public agenda?

84. Have more efficient (sensitive) and appropriate measures been adopted to respond to the political and socio-cultural problems identified?

85. Does the program have follow-up mechanisms (to verify the quality of the products, punctuality of delivery, etc.) to measure progress in the achievement of the envisaged results?

86. When will the MicroStrategy project be done?

87. How will it affect you?

88. Is the MicroStrategy project supported by national and/or local organizations?

89. To what extent has a PMO contributed to raising the quality of the design of the MicroStrategy project?

90. Does it make any difference if you are successful?

2.1 Project Management Plan: MicroStrategy

91. Is mitigation authorized or recommended?

92. Who is the MicroStrategy project Manager?

93. What went right?

94. If the MicroStrategy project is complex or scope is specialized, do you have appropriate and/or qualified staff available to perform the tasks?

95. What worked well?

96. Is the budget realistic?

97. What went wrong?

98. When is the MicroStrategy project management plan created?

99. Do there need to be organizational changes?

100. Will you add a schedule and diagram?

101. What are the deliverables?

102. Are the existing and future without-plan conditions reasonable and appropriate?

103. How do you manage time?

104. Are comparable cost estimates used for comparing, screening and selecting alternative plans, and has a reasonable cost estimate been developed for the recommended plan?

105. Are cost risk analysis methods applied to develop contingencies for the estimated total MicroStrategy project costs?

106. Are the proposed MicroStrategy project purposes different than a previously authorized MicroStrategy project?

107. What would you do differently?

108. Where does all this information come from?

109. Was the peer (technical) review of the cost estimates duly coordinated with the cost estimate center of expertise and addressed in the review documentation and certification?

110. What is the justification?

2.2 Scope Management Plan: MicroStrategy

111. What are the risks that could significantly affect the communication on the MicroStrategy project?

112. Is there a Steering Committee in place?

113. Are changes in scope (deliverable commitments) agreed to by all affected groups & individuals?

114. What is the estimated cost of creating and implementing?

115. Is there a MicroStrategy project organization chart showing the reporting relationships and responsibilities for each position?

116. Has a capability assessment been conducted?

117. Have all team members been part of identifying risks?

118. Were MicroStrategy project team members involved in detailed estimating and scheduling?

119. Do you have funding for MicroStrategy project and product development, implementation and on-going support?

120. Do you have the reasons why the changes to your organizational systems and capabilities are required?

121. What should you drop in order to add something new?

122. Are target dates established for each milestone deliverable?

123. Are multiple estimation methods being employed?

124. Are MicroStrategy project contact logs kept up to date?

125. Can the MicroStrategy project team do several activities in parallel?

126. Describe how the deliverables will be verified against the MicroStrategy project scope. To whom will the deliverables be first presented for inspection and verification?

127. Is there a set of procedures defining the scope, procedures, and deliverables defining quality control?

128. What are the risks of not having good inter-organization cooperation on the MicroStrategy project?

129. Are alternatives safe, functional, constructible, economical, reasonable and sustainable?

2.3 Requirements Management Plan: MicroStrategy

130. Subject to change control?

131. What is a problem?

132. Who is responsible for monitoring and tracking the MicroStrategy project requirements?

133. How detailed should the MicroStrategy project get?

134. Who will approve the requirements (and if multiple approvers, in what order)?

135. Describe the process for rejecting the MicroStrategy project requirements. Who has the authority to reject MicroStrategy project requirements?

136. When and how will a requirements baseline be established in this MicroStrategy project?

137. How will requirements be managed?

138. Do you really need to write this document at all?

139. Will the contractors involved take full responsibility?

140. Who will perform the analysis?

141. How will bidders price evaluations be done, by deliverables, phases, or in a big bang?

142. Is there formal agreement on who has authority to approve a change in requirements?

143. Are actual resources expenditures versus planned expenditures acceptable?

144. Did you avoid subjective, flowery or non-specific statements?

145. What is the earliest finish date for this MicroStrategy project if it is scheduled to start on ...?

146. Should you include sub-activities?

147. Is the system software (non-operating system) new to the IT MicroStrategy project team?

148. How will the requirements become prioritized?

149. What are you counting on?

2.4 Requirements Documentation: MicroStrategy

150. Have the benefits identified with the system being identified clearly?

151. Does the system provide the functions which best support the customers needs?

152. What are current process problems?

153. What are the attributes of a customer?

154. How linear / iterative is your Requirements Gathering process (or will it be)?

155. What variations exist for a process?

156. Where do you define what is a customer, what are the attributes of customer?

157. Are there legal issues?

158. What can tools do for us?

159. Basic work/business process; high-level, what is being touched?

160. Do technical resources exist?

161. How does what is being described meet the business need?

162. How will the proposed MicroStrategy project help?

163. What happens when requirements are wrong?

164. The problem with gathering requirements is right there in the word gathering. What images does it conjure?

165. What is the risk associated with the technology?

166. Where are business rules being captured?

167. How do you know when a Requirement is accurate enough?

168. How can you document system requirements?

169. Consistency. are there any requirements conflicts?

2.5 Requirements Traceability Matrix: MicroStrategy

170. What percentage of MicroStrategy projects are producing traceability matrices between requirements and other work products?

171. How small is small enough?

172. Is there a requirements traceability process in place?

173. How do you manage scope?

174. What is the WBS?

175. Will you use a Requirements Traceability Matrix?

176. Do you have a clear understanding of all subcontracts in place?

177. Describe the process for approving requirements so they can be added to the traceability matrix and MicroStrategy project work can be performed. Will the MicroStrategy project requirements become approved in writing?

178. Why use a WBS?

179. What are the chronologies, contingencies, consequences, criteria?

180. How will it affect the stakeholders personally in

career?

181. Why do you manage scope?

2.6 Project Scope Statement: MicroStrategy

182. Are there specific processes you will use to evaluate and approve/reject changes?

183. What actions will be taken to mitigate the risk?

184. Will an issue form be in use?

185. Will you need a statement of work?

186. Do you anticipate new stakeholders joining the MicroStrategy project over time?

187. How will you verify the accuracy of the work of the MicroStrategy project, and what constitutes acceptance of the deliverables?

188. Relevant - ask yourself can you get there; why are you doing this MicroStrategy project?

189. Write a brief purpose statement for this MicroStrategy project. Include a business justification statement. What is the product of this MicroStrategy project?

190. Is the scope of your MicroStrategy project well defined?

191. Will the MicroStrategy project risks be managed according to the MicroStrategy projects risk management process?

192. Did your MicroStrategy project ask for this?

193. Will there be a Change Control Process in place?

194. Is the plan under configuration management?

195. Is the MicroStrategy project manager qualified and experienced in MicroStrategy project management?

196. Once its defined, what is the stability of the MicroStrategy project scope?

197. What is the product of this MicroStrategy project?

198. Are there adequate MicroStrategy project control systems?

199. Elements that deal with providing the detail?

2.7 Assumption and Constraint Log: MicroStrategy

200. Can you perform this task or activity in a more effective manner?

201. Is this model reasonable?

202. What to do at recovery?

203. Is there adequate stakeholder participation for the vetting of requirements definition, changes and management?

204. If appropriate, is the deliverable content consistent with current MicroStrategy project documents and in compliance with the Document Management Plan?

205. When can log be discarded?

206. What would you gain if you spent time working to improve this process?

207. Are there ways to reduce the time it takes to get something approved?

208. What do you log?

209. How can you prevent/fix violations?

210. Is the steering committee active in MicroStrategy project oversight?

211. Was the document/deliverable developed per the appropriate or required standards (for example, Institute of Electrical and Electronics Engineers standards)?

212. What other teams / processes would be impacted by changes to the current process, and how?

213. Contradictory information between document sections?

214. Has a MicroStrategy project Communications Plan been developed?

215. Violation trace: why ?

216. Does the traceability documentation describe the tool and/or mechanism to be used to capture traceability throughout the life cycle?

217. Is the definition of the MicroStrategy project scope clear; what needs to be accomplished?

218. Does the system design reflect the requirements?

2.8 Work Breakdown Structure: MicroStrategy

219. How many levels?

220. Who has to do it?

221. Is it still viable?

222. What is the probability that the MicroStrategy project duration will exceed xx weeks?

223. How big is a work-package?

224. What has to be done?

225. When do you stop?

226. When would you develop a Work Breakdown Structure?

227. Is It a change in scope?

228. Is the work breakdown structure (wbs) defined and is the scope of the MicroStrategy project clear with assigned deliverable owners?

229. Why is it useful?

230. What is the probability of completing the MicroStrategy project in less that xx days?

231. Do you need another level?

232. How much detail?

233. Where does it take place?

234. When does it have to be done?

2.9 WBS Dictionary: MicroStrategy

235. Are direct or indirect cost adjustments being accomplished according to accounting procedures acceptable to us?

236. Does the contractors system include procedures for measuring performance of the lowest level organization responsible for the control account?

237. Is all contract work included in the CWBS?

238. Are meaningful indicators identified for use in measuring the status of cost and schedule performance?

239. Does the contractors system provide for accurate cost accumulation and assignment to control accounts in a manner consistent with the budgets using recognized acceptable costing techniques?

240. Are current budgets resulting from changes to the authorized work and/or internal replanning, reconcilable to original budgets for specified reporting items?

241. Are overhead cost budgets established for each organization which has authority to incur overhead costs?

242. The anticipated business volume?

243. Are records maintained to show full accountability for all material purchased for the

contract, including the residual inventory?

244. Is subcontracted work defined and identified to the appropriate subcontractor within the proper WBS element?

245. Is cost and schedule performance measurement done in a consistent, systematic manner?

246. Is future work which cannot be planned in detail subdivided to the extent practicable for budgeting and scheduling purposes?

247. Are the contractors estimates of costs at completion reconcilable with cost data reported to us?

248. Time-phased control account budgets?

249. Do work packages consist of discrete tasks which are adequately described?

250. Does the scheduling system identify in a timely manner the status of work?

251. Are significant decision points, constraints, and interfaces identified as key milestones?

252. Does the contractor require sufficient detailed planning of control accounts to constrain the application of budget initially allocated for future effort to current effort?

2.10 Schedule Management Plan: MicroStrategy

253. Who is responsible for estimating the activity durations?

254. Is the ims development and management approach described?

255. Have the procedures for identifying budget variances been followed?

256. Does the resource management plan include a personnel development plan?

257. Has process improvement efforts been completed before requirements efforts begin?

258. Is funded schedule margin reasonable and logically distributed?

259. Is there a procedure for management, control and release of schedule margin?

260. Is there a requirements change management processes in place?

261. Has your organization readiness assessment been conducted?

262. Has a structured approach been used to break work effort into manageable components (WBS)?

263. Has the MicroStrategy project manager been identified?

264. Are the people assigned to the MicroStrategy project sufficiently qualified?

265. Perform reality checks on schedules – are all tasks included?

266. Is a pmo (MicroStrategy project management office) in place and provide oversight to the MicroStrategy project?

267. Have MicroStrategy project management standards and procedures been identified / established and documented?

268. Must the MicroStrategy project be complete by a specified date?

269. Has the schedule been baselined?

270. Are the MicroStrategy project plans updated on a frequent basis?

271. Does the MicroStrategy project have quality set of schedule BOEs?

272. Are the processes for schedule assessment and analysis defined?

2.11 Activity List: MicroStrategy

273. What are the critical bottleneck activities?

274. What is the probability the MicroStrategy project can be completed in xx weeks?

275. How do you determine the late start (LS) for each activity?

276. Can you determine the activity that must finish, before this activity can start?

277. What went well?

278. Where will it be performed?

279. How can the MicroStrategy project be displayed graphically to better visualize the activities?

280. The wbs is developed as part of a joint planning session, and how do you know that youhave done this right?

281. Is infrastructure setup part of your MicroStrategy project?

282. Are the required resources available or need to be acquired?

283. How difficult will it be to do specific activities on this MicroStrategy project?

284. What is your organizations history in doing

similar activities?

285. Is there anything planned that does not need to be here?

286. For other activities, how much delay can be tolerated?

287. When will the work be performed?

288. What is the total time required to complete the MicroStrategy project if no delays occur?

289. How will it be performed?

290. When do the individual activities need to start and finish?

2.12 Activity Attributes: MicroStrategy

291. What activity do you think you should spend the most time on?

292. Can more resources be added?

293. Why?

294. How many resources do you need to complete the work scope within a limit of X number of days?

295. How much activity detail is required?

296. Does your organization of the data change its meaning?

297. Resources to accomplish the work?

298. Activity: what is In the Bag?

299. Would you consider either of corresponding activities an outlier?

300. How else could the items be grouped?

301. Are the required resources available?

302. Where else does it apply?

303. How difficult will it be to do specific activities on this MicroStrategy project?

304. Time for overtime?

2.13 Milestone List: MicroStrategy

305. How will the milestone be verified?

306. Own known vulnerabilities?

307. How will you get the word out to customers?

308. Continuity, supply chain robustness?

309. Calculate how long can activity be delayed?

310. Legislative effects?

311. What has been done so far?

312. Environmental effects?

313. Can you derive how soon can the whole MicroStrategy project finish?

314. New USPs?

315. Sustainable financial backing?

316. Describe the industry you are in and the market growth opportunities. What is the market for your technology, product or service?

317. Identify critical paths (one or more) and which activities are on the critical path?

318. Usps (unique selling points)?

319. What would happen if a delivery of material was one week late?

320. Do you foresee any technical risks or developmental challenges?

321. How late can the activity finish?

322. What specific improvements did you make to the MicroStrategy project proposal since the previous time?

323. Which path is the critical path?

2.14 Network Diagram: MicroStrategy

324. What activity must be completed immediately before this activity can start?

325. If a current contract exists, can you provide the vendor name, contract start, and contract expiration date?

326. What is the lowest cost to complete this MicroStrategy project in xx weeks?

327. Can you calculate the confidence level?

328. Where do you schedule uncertainty time?

329. How difficult will it be to do specific activities on this MicroStrategy project?

330. What controls the start and finish of a job?

331. Are you on time?

332. What job or jobs follow it?

333. Which type of network diagram allows you to depict four types of dependencies?

334. What activities must occur simultaneously with this activity?

335. What is the completion time?

336. What are the Major Administrative Issues?

337. Will crashing x weeks return more in benefits than it costs?

338. What activities must follow this activity?

339. What can be done concurrently?

340. How confident can you be in your milestone dates and the delivery date?

2.15 Activity Resource Requirements: MicroStrategy

341. What are constraints that you might find during the Human Resource Planning process?

342. When does monitoring begin?

343. How many signatures do you require on a check and does this match what is in your policy and procedures?

344. Other support in specific areas?

345. Anything else?

346. Do you use tools like decomposition and rolling-wave planning to produce the activity list and other outputs?

347. Which logical relationship does the PDM use most often?

348. Why do you do that?

349. Are there unresolved issues that need to be addressed?

350. How do you handle petty cash?

351. What is the Work Plan Standard?

352. Organizational Applicability?

2.16 Resource Breakdown Structure: MicroStrategy

353. Which resources should be in the resource pool?

354. What can you do to improve productivity?

355. How difficult will it be to do specific activities on this MicroStrategy project?

356. What defines a successful MicroStrategy project?

357. What is each stakeholders desired outcome for the MicroStrategy project?

358. Any changes from stakeholders?

359. When do they need the information?

360. Who delivers the information?

361. Is predictive resource analysis being done?

362. What are the requirements for resource data?

363. Which resource planning tool provides information on resource responsibility and accountability?

364. What is the primary purpose of the human resource plan?

365. What is the difference between % Complete and

% work?

366. The list could probably go on, but, the thing that you would most like to know is, How long & How much?

367. How should the information be delivered?

2.17 Activity Duration Estimates: MicroStrategy

368. Is evaluation criteria defined to rate proposals?

369. What is the duration of the critical path for this MicroStrategy project?

370. Are procedures defined for calculating cost estimates?

371. Does the software appear easy to learn?

372. Will it help promote wellness at your organization and reduce insurance costs?

373. Which skills do you think are most important for an information technology MicroStrategy project manager?

374. What functions does this software provide that cannot be done easily using other tools such as a spreadsheet or database?

375. MicroStrategy project manager has received activity duration estimates from his team. Which does one need in order to complete schedule development?

376. What MicroStrategy project was the first to use modern MicroStrategy project management?

377. Is a contract change control system defined to

manage changes to contract terms and conditions?

378. Who will promote it?

379. Which includes asking team members about the time estimates for activities and reaching agreement on the calendar date for each activity?

380. Do MicroStrategy project team members work in the same physical location to enhance team performance?

381. What are some general rules of thumb for deciding if cost variance, schedule variance, cost performance index, and schedule performance index numbers are good or bad?

382. Why do you need a good WBS to use MicroStrategy project management software?

383. Does a process exist to formally recognize new MicroStrategy projects?

384. Which is a benefit of an analogous MicroStrategy project estimate?

385. Are operational definitions created to identify quality measurement criteria for specific activities?

386. Consider the common sources of risk on information technology MicroStrategy projects and suggestions for managing them. Which suggestions do you find most useful?

387. Do scope statements include the MicroStrategy project objectives and expected deliverables?

2.18 Duration Estimating Worksheet: MicroStrategy

388. What work will be included in the MicroStrategy project?

389. What is the total time required to complete the MicroStrategy project if no delays occur?

390. How should ongoing costs be monitored to try to keep the MicroStrategy project within budget?

391. What is next?

392. Is this operation cost effective?

393. Does the MicroStrategy project provide innovative ways for stakeholders to overcome obstacles or deliver better outcomes?

394. Small or large MicroStrategy project?

395. What questions do you have?

396. Can the MicroStrategy project be constructed as planned?

397. Do any colleagues have experience with your organization and/or RFPs?

398. Why estimate time and cost?

399. Why estimate costs?

400. What utility impacts are there?

401. What info is needed?

402. What is an Average MicroStrategy project?

403. Will the MicroStrategy project collaborate with the local community and leverage resources?

404. Define the work as completely as possible. What work will be included in the MicroStrategy project?

2.19 Project Schedule: MicroStrategy

405. Are there activities that came from a template or previous MicroStrategy project that are not applicable on this phase of this MicroStrategy project?

406. Are all remaining durations correct?

407. It allows the MicroStrategy project to be delivered on schedule. How Do you Use Schedules?

408. Are the original MicroStrategy project schedule and budget realistic?

409. Are quality inspections and review activities listed in the MicroStrategy project schedule(s)?

410. How effectively were issues able to be resolved without impacting the MicroStrategy project Schedule or Budget?

411. Eliminate unnecessary activities. Are there activities that came from a template or previous MicroStrategy project that are not applicable on this phase of this MicroStrategy project?

412. Did the MicroStrategy project come in on schedule?

413. How can you address that situation?

414. Your best shot for providing estimations how complex/how much work does the activity require?

415. Meet requirements?

416. Why or why not?

417. Activity charts and bar charts are graphical representations of a MicroStrategy project schedule ...how do they differ?

418. Was the MicroStrategy project schedule reviewed by all stakeholders and formally accepted?

419. If there are any qualifying green components to this MicroStrategy project, what portion of the total MicroStrategy project cost is green?

420. MicroStrategy project work estimates Who is managing the work estimate quality of work tasks in the MicroStrategy project schedule?

421. Are you working on the right risks?

422. How does a MicroStrategy project get to be a year late ?

423. Is infrastructure setup part of your MicroStrategy project?

2.20 Cost Management Plan: MicroStrategy

424. Are the people assigned to the MicroStrategy project sufficiently qualified?

425. Is MicroStrategy project status reviewed with the steering and executive teams at appropriate intervals?

426. Is there an onboarding process in place?

427. Is there anything unique in this MicroStrategy projects scope statement that will affect resources?

428. Are mitigation strategies identified?

429. Do MicroStrategy project teams & team members report on status / activities / progress?

430. Have adequate resources been provided by management to ensure MicroStrategy project success?

431. Are actuals compared against estimates to analyze and correct variances?

432. Are all payments made according to the contract(s)?

433. Timeline and milestones?

434. How does the proposed individual meet each requirement?

435. Has a MicroStrategy project Communications Plan been developed?

436. Are status reports received per the MicroStrategy project Plan?

437. Does the MicroStrategy project have a Statement of Work?

438. How do you manage cost?

439. Was the MicroStrategy project schedule reviewed by all stakeholders and formally accepted?

440. Quality assurance overheads?

441. Risk Analysis?

442. Has the business need been clearly defined?

2.21 Activity Cost Estimates: MicroStrategy

443. How do you fund change orders?

444. What procedures are put in place regarding bidding and cost comparisons, if any?

445. Does the estimator estimate by task or by person?

446. Performance bond should always provide what part of the contract value?

447. Can you change your activities?

448. How difficult will it be to do specific tasks on the MicroStrategy project?

449. Who determines when the contractor is paid?

450. Can you delete activities or make them inactive?

451. Was it performed on time?

452. What do you want to know about the stay to know if costs were inappropriately high or low?

453. What defines a successful MicroStrategy project?

454. What is the estimators estimating history?

455. What cost data should be used to estimate costs

during the 2-year follow-up period?

456. What is included in indirect cost being allocated?

457. What happens if you cannot produce the documentation for the single audit?

458. What is the activity inventory?

459. Does the activity rely on a common set of tools to carry it out?

2.22 Cost Estimating Worksheet: MicroStrategy

460. What additional MicroStrategy project(s) could be initiated as a result of this MicroStrategy project?

461. What is the purpose of estimating?

462. What will others want?

463. What costs are to be estimated?

464. Will the MicroStrategy project collaborate with the local community and leverage resources?

465. Identify the timeframe necessary to monitor progress and collect data to determine how the selected measure has changed?

466. Value pocket identification & quantification what are value pockets?

467. What can be included?

468. Does the MicroStrategy project provide innovative ways for stakeholders to overcome obstacles or deliver better outcomes?

469. How will the results be shared and to whom?

470. Can a trend be established from historical performance data on the selected measure and are the criteria for using trend analysis or forecasting

methods met?

471. Is it feasible to establish a control group arrangement?

472. Is the MicroStrategy project responsive to community need?

473. Who is best positioned to know and assist in identifying corresponding factors?

474. What is the estimated labor cost today based upon this information?

475. What happens to any remaining funds not used?

476. Ask: are others positioned to know, are others credible, and will others cooperate?

2.23 Cost Baseline: MicroStrategy

477. Have the lessons learned been filed with the MicroStrategy project Management Office?

478. What is the reality?

479. On time?

480. Has the actual cost of the MicroStrategy project (or MicroStrategy project phase) been tallied and compared to the approved budget?

481. What strengths do you have?

482. Escalation criteria met?

483. Has the MicroStrategy projected annual cost to operate and maintain the product(s) or service(s) been approved and funded?

484. When should cost estimates be developed?

485. How will cost estimates be used?

486. Will the MicroStrategy project fail if the change request is not executed?

487. Have all approved changes to the schedule baseline been identified and impact on the MicroStrategy project documented?

488. Is there anything unique in this MicroStrategy projects scope statement that will affect resources?

489. What threats might prevent you from getting there?

490. What is your organizations history in doing similar tasks?

491. Has the MicroStrategy project (or MicroStrategy project phase) been evaluated against each objective established in the product description and Integrated MicroStrategy project Plan?

492. What is the most important thing to do next to make your MicroStrategy project successful?

493. Does the suggested change request seem to represent a necessary enhancement to the product?

494. Where do changes come from?

2.24 Quality Management Plan: MicroStrategy

495. How are senior leaders, employees, and your organization involved in supporting the community?

496. How does your organization decide what to measure?

497. Who needs a qmp?

498. What field records are generated?

499. Do you keep back-up copies of any data?

500. What data do you gather/use/compile?

501. How do you ensure that your sampling methods and procedures meet your data needs?

502. Has a MicroStrategy project Communications Plan been developed?

503. How is staff trained in procedures?

504. How will you know that a change is actually an improvement?

505. When reporting to different audiences, do you vary the form or type of report?

506. How does the material compare to a regulatory threshold?

507. Have you eliminated all duplicative tasks or manual efforts, where appropriate?

508. How is the information recorded?

509. What is the return on investment?

510. No superfluous information or marketing narrative?

511. How do senior leaders create and communicate values and performance expectations?

512. Who do you send data to?

513. Does the program use modeling in the permitting or decision-making processes?

2.25 Quality Metrics: MicroStrategy

514. Is material complete (and does it meet the standards)?

515. What approved evidence based screening tools can be used?

516. What are your organizations expectations for its quality MicroStrategy project?

517. Filter visualizations of interest?

518. Why is now the time for quality metrics?

519. What metrics do you measure?

520. Which are the right metrics to use?

521. How does one achieve stability?

522. What percentage are outcome-based?

523. Are interface issues coordinated?

524. Is there alignment within your organization on definitions?

525. What group is empowered to define quality requirements?

526. What method of measurement do you use?

527. Have risk areas been identified?

528. Are there any open risk issues?

529. What can manufacturing professionals do to ensure quality is seen as an integral part of the entire product lifecycle?

530. How do you calculate such metrics?

531. How should customers provide input?

532. Is a risk containment plan in place?

533. What happens if you get an abnormal result?

2.26 Process Improvement Plan: MicroStrategy

534. Why quality management?

535. Has a process guide to collect the data been developed?

536. Has the time line required to move measurement results from the points of collection to databases or users been established?

537. Purpose of goal: the motive is determined by asking, why do you want to achieve this goal?

538. Are there forms and procedures to collect and record the data?

539. The motive is determined by asking, Why do you want to achieve this goal?

540. Where do you want to be?

541. Have storage and access mechanisms and procedures been determined?

542. Are you making progress on the goals?

543. What personnel are the coaches for your initiative?

544. Are you following the quality standards?

545. Does explicit definition of the measures exist?

546. Have the frequency of collection and the points in the process where measurements will be made been determined?

547. How do you measure?

548. If a process improvement framework is being used, which elements will help the problems and goals listed?

549. Management commitment at all levels?

550. Where are you now?

551. What personnel are the champions for the initiative?

552. Does your process ensure quality?

2.27 Responsibility Assignment Matrix: MicroStrategy

553. Major functional areas of contract effort?

554. Is it safe to say you can handle more work or that some tasks you are supposed to do arent worth doing?

555. Are the overhead pools formally and adequately identified?

556. What do you need to implement earned value management?

557. No rs: if a task has no one listed as responsible, who is getting the job done?

558. Is work properly classified as measured effort, LOE, or apportioned effort and appropriately separated?

559. Does the contractors system identify work accomplishment against the schedule plan?

560. Authorization to proceed with all authorized work?

561. Do managers and team members provide helpful suggestions during review meetings?

562. What tool can show you individual and group allocations?

563. Identify and isolate causes of favorable and unfavorable cost and schedule variances?

564. The staff interests – is the group or the person interested in working for this MicroStrategy project?

565. All cwbs elements specified for external reporting?

566. With too many people labeled as doing the work, are there too many hands involved?

567. Are records maintained to show how undistributed budgets are controlled?

568. Is budgeted cost for work performed calculated in a manner consistent with the way work is planned?

569. What expertise is available in your department?

2.28 Roles and Responsibilities: MicroStrategy

570. Be specific; avoid generalities. Thank you and great work alone are insufficient. What exactly do you appreciate and why?

571. What should you do now to ensure that you are meeting all expectations of your current position?

572. Who is involved?

573. How is your work-life balance?

574. Implementation of actions: Who are the responsible units?

575. To decide whether to use a quality measurement, ask how will you know when it is achieved?

576. What expectations were NOT met?

577. Are governance roles and responsibilities documented?

578. What should you highlight for improvement?

579. Once the responsibilities are defined for the MicroStrategy project, have the deliverables, roles and responsibilities been clearly communicated to every participant?

580. Is there a training program in place for

stakeholders covering expectations, roles and responsibilities and any addition knowledge others need to be good stakeholders?

581. Concern: where are you limited or have no authority, where you can not influence?

582. What are your major roles and responsibilities in the area of performance measurement and assessment?

583. Was the expectation clearly communicated?

584. Accountabilities: what are the roles and responsibilities of individual team members?

585. Do you take the time to clearly define roles and responsibilities on MicroStrategy project tasks?

586. Are your policies supportive of a culture of quality data?

587. Are the quality assurance functions and related roles and responsibilities clearly defined?

588. Is the data complete?

589. Are MicroStrategy project team roles and responsibilities identified and documented?

2.29 Human Resource Management Plan: MicroStrategy

590. What were things that you did very well and want to do the same again on the next MicroStrategy project?

591. List the assumptions made to date. What did you have to assume to be true to complete the charter?

592. Is your organization certified as a supplier, wholesaler, regular dealer, or manufacturer of corresponding products/supplies?

593. Does the detailed work plan match the complexity of tasks with the capabilities of personnel?

594. What areas were overlooked on this MicroStrategy project?

595. Have lessons learned been conducted after each MicroStrategy project release?

596. How do you determine what key skills and talents are needed to meet the objectives. Is your organization primarily focused on a specific industry?

597. Have the key functions and capabilities been defined and assigned to each release or iteration?

598. Are risk triggers captured?

599. Are quality metrics defined?

600. Is MicroStrategy project status reviewed with the steering and executive teams at appropriate intervals?

601. Has the scope management document been updated and distributed to help prevent scope creep?

602. Is documentation created for communication with the suppliers and Vendors?

603. What did you have to assume to be true to complete the charter?

604. Is it standard practice to formally commit stakeholders to the MicroStrategy project via agreements?

605. Are there checklists created to determine if all quality processes are followed?

2.30 Communications Management Plan: MicroStrategy

606. How will the person responsible for executing the communication item be notified?

607. Who is involved as you identify stakeholders?

608. Are others part of the communications management plan?

609. Do you then often overlook a key stakeholder or stakeholder group?

610. What data is going to be required?

611. Which team member will work with each stakeholder?

612. Who did you turn to if you had questions?

613. Will messages be directly related to the release strategy or phases of the MicroStrategy project?

614. What is the political influence?

615. Which stakeholders can influence others?

616. Who were proponents/opponents?

617. Which stakeholders are thought leaders, influences, or early adopters?

618. Are there potential barriers between the team and the stakeholder?

619. Do you have members of your team responsible for certain stakeholders?

620. Who will use or be affected by the result of a MicroStrategy project?

621. Do you prepare stakeholder engagement plans?

622. Is there an important stakeholder who is actively opposed and will not receive messages?

623. Why is stakeholder engagement important?

624. What does the stakeholder need from the team?

2.31 Risk Management Plan: MicroStrategy

625. Are requirements fully understood by the software engineering team and customers?

626. Are flexibility and reuse paramount?

627. Are team members trained in the use of the tools?

628. What can go wrong?

629. Monitoring -what factors can you track that will enable you to determine if the risk is becoming more or less likely?

630. What are it-specific requirements?

631. How is risk identification performed?

632. Are the reports useful and easy to read?

633. Risk probability and impact: how will the probabilities and impacts of risk items be assessed?

634. How quickly does this item need to be resolved?

635. What can you do to minimize the impact if it does?

636. Is the process being followed?

637. Do you train all developers in the process?

638. Do you manage the process through use of metrics?

639. What should be done with non-critical risks?

640. Does the software engineering team have the right mix of skills?

641. Are the metrics meaningful and useful?

642. Is this an issue, action item, question or a risk?

643. How will the MicroStrategy project know if your organizations risk response actions were effective?

644. Are people attending meetings and doing work?

2.32 Risk Register: MicroStrategy

645. What evidence do you have to justify the likelihood score of the risk (audit, incident report, claim, complaints, inspection, internal review)?

646. Amongst the action plans and recommendations that you have to introduce are there some that could stop or delay the overall program?

647. What action, if any, has been taken to respond to the risk?

648. Why would you develop a risk register?

649. When would you develop a risk register?

650. Methodology: how will risk management be performed on this MicroStrategy project?

651. Are there any knock-on effects/impact on any of the other areas?

652. What further options might be available for responding to the risk?

653. Is further information required before making a decision?

654. Preventative actions - planned actions to reduce the likelihood a risk will occur and/or reduce the seriousness should it occur. What should you do now?

655. How is a Community Risk Register created?

656. Financial risk -can your organization afford to undertake the MicroStrategy project?

657. What are you going to do to limit the MicroStrategy projects risk exposure due to the identified risks?

658. Do you require further engagement?

659. Having taken action, how did the responses effect change, and where is the MicroStrategy project now?

660. What are the main aims, objectives of the policy, strategy, or service and the intended outcomes?

661. Market risk -will the new service or product be useful to your organization or marketable to others?

662. When will it happen?

663. What risks might negatively or positively affect achieving the MicroStrategy project objectives?

2.33 Probability and Impact Assessment: MicroStrategy

664. Do the people have the right combinations of skills?

665. Is the customer willing to commit significant time to the requirements gathering process?

666. Who should be notified of the occurrence of each of the risk indicators?

667. What kind of preparation would be required to do this?

668. What is the impact if the risk does occur?

669. What significant shift will occur in governmental policies, laws, and regulations pertaining to specific industries?

670. Who has experience with this?

671. Have customers been involved fully in the definition of requirements?

672. Costs associated with late delivery or a defective product?

673. Risk urgency assessment -which of your risks could occur soon, or require a longer planning time?

674. What are the channels available for distribution

to the customer?

675. Does the MicroStrategy project team have experience with the technology to be implemented?

676. What are the tools and techniques used in managing the challenges faced?

677. What risks are necessary to achieve success?

678. What are its business ethics?

679. How is risk handled within this MicroStrategy project organization?

680. Is the MicroStrategy project cutting across the entire organization?

681. Would avoiding any of corresponding impact the MicroStrategy projects chance of success?

682. How carefully have the potential competitors been identified?

2.34 Probability and Impact Matrix: MicroStrategy

683. Does the customer have a solid idea of what is required?

684. Which role do you have in the MicroStrategy project?

685. What is the likelihood of a breakthrough?

686. Can you handle the investment risk?

687. What can possibly go wrong?

688. What would be the best solution?

689. Can you stabilize dynamic risk factors?

690. How solid are the price-volume MicroStrategy projections?

691. Are you on schedule?

692. What will be the likely political environment during the life of the MicroStrategy project?

693. Is the present organizational structure for handling the MicroStrategy project sufficient?

694. Pay attention to the quality of the plans: is the content complete, or does it seem to be lacking detail?

695. What will be the environmental impact of the MicroStrategy project?

696. If you can not fix it, how do you do it differently?

697. Has the need for the MicroStrategy project been properly established?

698. What will be the likely political situation during the life of the MicroStrategy project?

699. How completely has the customer been identified?

700. Are compilers and code generators available and suitable for the product to be built?

701. Workarounds are determined during which risk management process?

2.35 Risk Data Sheet: MicroStrategy

702. What are you weak at and therefore need to do better?

703. Has the most cost-effective solution been chosen?

704. What are you trying to achieve (Objectives)?

705. Has a sensitivity analysis been carried out?

706. What can you do?

707. How reliable is the data source?

708. Potential for recurrence?

709. What are you here for (Mission)?

710. Will revised controls lead to tolerable risk levels?

711. What do you know?

712. Who has a vested interest in how you perform as your organization (our stakeholders)?

713. Whom do you serve (customers)?

714. Risk of what?

715. How do you handle product safely?

716. What is the chance that it will happen?

717. What are the main opportunities available to you that you should grab while you can?

718. What is the environment within which you operate (social trends, economic, community values, broad based participation, national directions etc.)?

719. How can hazards be reduced?

720. What if client refuses?

2.36 Procurement Management Plan: MicroStrategy

721. What are you trying to accomplish?

722. Are internal MicroStrategy project status meetings held at reasonable intervals?

723. Is a stakeholder management plan in place that covers topics?

724. Are status reports received per the MicroStrategy project Plan?

725. Is quality monitored from the perspective of the customers needs and expectations?

726. Have stakeholder accountabilities & responsibilities been clearly defined?

727. Are the people assigned to the MicroStrategy project sufficiently qualified?

728. Are tasks tracked by hours?

729. What were things that you did well, and could improve, and how?

730. How will multiple providers be managed?

731. Are key risk mitigation strategies added to the MicroStrategy project schedule?

732. Is there a formal set of procedures supporting Issues Management?

733. Have adequate resources been provided by management to ensure MicroStrategy project success?

734. Are the appropriate IT resources adequate to meet planned commitments?

735. Is there a procurement management plan in place?

736. Was the MicroStrategy project schedule reviewed by all stakeholders and formally accepted?

737. Is pert / critical path or equivalent methodology being used?

738. Is the structure for tracking the MicroStrategy project schedule well defined and assigned to a specific individual?

2.37 Source Selection Criteria: MicroStrategy

739. Have all evaluators been trained?

740. Who must be notified?

741. Is a letter of commitment from each proposed team member and key subcontractor included?

742. What will you use to capture evaluation and subsequent documentation?

743. Is there collaboration among your evaluators?

744. How should comments received in response to a RFP be handled?

745. What benefits are accrued from issuing a DRFP in advance of issuing a final RFP?

746. Are evaluators ready to begin this task?

747. How much past performance information should be requested?

748. What does a sample rating scale look like?

749. Do you ensure you evaluate what you asked for, not what you want to see or expect to see?

750. What are the requirements for publicizing a RFP?

751. In which phase of the acquisition process cycle does source qualifications reside?

752. Can you make a cost/technical tradeoff?

753. Does your documentation identify why the team concurs or differs with reported performance from past performance report (CPARs, questionnaire responses, etc.)?

754. With the rapid changes in information technology, will media be readable in five or ten years?

755. What procedures are followed when a contractor requires access to classified information or a significant quantity of special material/information?

756. How should the solicitation aspects regarding past performance be structured?

757. Do you have a plan to document consensus results including disposition of any disagreement by individual evaluators?

758. Will the technical evaluation factor unnecessarily force the acquisition into a higher-priced market segment?

2.38 Stakeholder Management Plan: MicroStrategy

759. Are enough systems & user personnel assigned to the MicroStrategy project?

760. What action will be taken once reports have been received?

761. Are there checklists created to demine if all quality processes are followed?

762. Are procurement deliverables arriving on time and to specification?

763. What is meant by activity dependencies and how do they relate to network diagramming?

764. Are staff skills known and available for each task?

765. Are updated MicroStrategy project time & resource estimates reasonable based on the current MicroStrategy project stage?

766. Have all stakeholders been identified?

767. What specific resources will be required for implementation activities?

768. What is the drawback in using qualitative MicroStrategy project selection techniques?

769. Alignment to strategic goals & objectives?

770. What information should be collected?

771. Is the communication plan being followed?

2.39 Change Management Plan: MicroStrategy

772. How badly can information be misinterpreted?

773. Will the culture embrace or reject this change?

774. What tasks are needed?

775. Have the systems been configured and tested?

776. Has the target training audience been identified and nominated?

777. When developing your communication plan do you address : When should the given message be communicated?

778. Has the relevant business unit been notified of installation and support requirements?

779. What prerequisite knowledge or training is required?

780. Who will fund the training?

781. What are the major changes to processes?

782. What is the reason for the communication?

783. Who should be involved in developing a change management strategy?

784. What processes are in place to manage knowledge about the MicroStrategy project?

785. Why is it important?

786. Where will the funds come from?

787. Who is the target audience of the piece of information?

788. Clearly articulate the overall business benefits of the MicroStrategy project -why are you doing this now?

789. Who in the business it includes?

790. What is the negative impact of communicating too soon or too late?

3.0 Executing Process Group: MicroStrategy

791. What business situation is being addressed?

792. What are the critical steps involved with strategy mapping?

793. Does the MicroStrategy project team have the right skills?

794. How will professionals learn what is expected from them what the deliverables are?

795. What factors are contributing to progress or delay in the achievement of products and results?

796. Who will be the main sponsor?

797. What type of information goes in the quality assurance plan?

798. What is the shortest possible time it will take to complete this MicroStrategy project?

799. When is the appropriate time to bring the scorecard to Board meetings?

800. How can your organization use a weighted decision matrix to evaluate proposals as part of source selection?

801. How do you control progress of your

MicroStrategy project?

802. How does the job market and current state of the economy affect human resource management?

803. How well did the chosen processes fit the needs of the MicroStrategy project?

804. What MicroStrategy projects and services are in the portfolio of your organization?

805. When do you share the scorecard with managers?

806. How is MicroStrategy project performance information created and distributed?

807. What is in place for ensuring adequate change control on MicroStrategy projects that involve outside contracts?

808. How can software assist in procuring goods and services?

809. Based on your MicroStrategy project communication management plan, what worked well?

3.1 Team Member Status Report: MicroStrategy

810. Does the product, good, or service already exist within your organization?

811. Does your organization have the means (staff, money, contract, etc.) to produce or to acquire the product, good, or service?

812. How does this product, good, or service meet the needs of the MicroStrategy project and your organization as a whole?

813. How will resource planning be done?

814. How it is to be done?

815. The problem with Reward & Recognition Programs is that the truly deserving people all too often get left out. How can you make it practical?

816. What specific interest groups do you have in place?

817. Why is it to be done?

818. Does every department have to have a MicroStrategy project Manager on staff?

819. Are your organizations MicroStrategy projects more successful over time?

820. Do you have an Enterprise MicroStrategy project Management Office (EPMO)?

821. What is to be done?

822. Are the products of your organizations MicroStrategy projects meeting customers objectives?

823. Will the staff do training or is that done by a third party?

824. How much risk is involved?

825. Are the attitudes of staff regarding MicroStrategy project work improving?

826. How can you make it practical?

827. Is there evidence that staff is taking a more professional approach toward management of your organizations MicroStrategy projects?

828. When a teams productivity and success depend on collaboration and the efficient flow of information, what generally fails them?

3.2 Change Request: MicroStrategy

829. Should a more thorough impact analysis be conducted?

830. Is it feasible to use requirements attributes as predictors of reliability?

831. Who is included in the change control team?

832. Can static requirements change attributes like the size of the change be used to predict reliability in execution?

833. Why were your requested changes rejected or not made?

834. Which requirements attributes affect the risk to reliability the most?

835. What kind of information about the change request needs to be captured?

836. Screen shots or attachments included in a Change Request?

837. What are the duties of the change control team?

838. Since there are no change requests in your MicroStrategy project at this point, what must you have before you begin?

839. Who is responsible for the implementation and monitoring of all measures?

840. Why control change across the life cycle?

841. What are the requirements for urgent changes?

842. How are the measures for carrying out the change established?

843. Will there be a change request form in use?

844. Customer acceptance plan how will the customer verify the change has been implemented successfully?

845. How many lines of code must be changed to implement the change?

846. What mechanism is used to appraise others of changes that are made?

847. What should be regulated in a change control operating instruction?

848. Should staff call into the helpdesk or go to the website?

3.3 Change Log: MicroStrategy

849. When was the request submitted?

850. Is the change backward compatible without limitations?

851. Is the submitted change a new change or a modification of a previously approved change?

852. Does the suggested change request represent a desired enhancement to the products functionality?

853. Will the MicroStrategy project fail if the change request is not executed?

854. Is the change request open, closed or pending?

855. Is the change request within MicroStrategy project scope?

856. Is this a mandatory replacement?

857. Who initiated the change request?

858. Is the requested change request a result of changes in other MicroStrategy project(s)?

859. How does this change affect the timeline of the schedule?

860. How does this change affect scope?

861. Do the described changes impact on the

integrity or security of the system?

862. When was the request approved?

863. How does this relate to the standards developed for specific business processes?

3.4 Decision Log: MicroStrategy

864. Linked to original objective?

865. With whom was the decision shared or considered?

866. What alternatives/risks were considered?

867. Who will be given a copy of this document and where will it be kept?

868. How consolidated and comprehensive a story can you tell by capturing currently available incident data in a central location and through a log of key decisions during an incident?

869. At what point in time does loss become unacceptable?

870. Is your opponent open to a non-traditional workflow, or will it likely challenge anything you do?

871. Do strategies and tactics aimed at less than full control reduce the costs of management or simply shift the cost burden?

872. What are the cost implications?

873. What eDiscovery problem or issue did your organization set out to fix or make better?

874. Behaviors; what are guidelines that the team has identified that will assist them with getting the most

out of team meetings?

875. Who is the decisionmaker?

876. How effective is maintaining the log at facilitating organizational learning?

877. What is the line where eDiscovery ends and document review begins?

878. Does anything need to be adjusted?

879. Decision-making process; how will the team make decisions?

880. What was the rationale for the decision?

881. How does provision of information, both in terms of content and presentation, influence acceptance of alternative strategies?

882. How does the use a Decision Support System influence the strategies/tactics or costs?

883. What is your overall strategy for quality control / quality assurance procedures?

3.5 Quality Audit: MicroStrategy

884. Are goals well supported with strategies, operational plans, manuals and training?

885. How does your organization know that its system for attending to the health and wellbeing of its staff is appropriately effective and constructive?

886. How does your organization know that its Governance system is appropriately effective and constructive?

887. How does your organization know that its system for attending to the particular needs of its international staff is appropriately effective and constructive?

888. Quality is about improvement and accountability. The immediate questions that arise out of that statement are: (i) improvement on what, and (ii) accountable to whom?

889. How does your organization know that the support for its staff is appropriately effective and constructive?

890. Are the review comments incorporated?

891. How does your organization know that its quality of teaching is appropriately effective and constructive?

892. Does the audit organization have experience in

performing the required work for entities of your type and size?

893. How does your organization know that its systems for assisting staff with career planning and employment placements are appropriately effective and constructive?

894. For each device to be reconditioned, are device specifications, such as appropriate engineering drawings, component specifications and software specifications, maintained?

895. How does your organization know that it is appropriately effective and constructive in preparing its staff for organizational aspirations?

896. Are measuring and test equipment that have been placed out of service suitably identified and excluded from use in any device reconditioning operation?

897. How does your organization know that its planning processes are appropriately effective and constructive?

898. Are the policies and processes, as set out in the Quality Audit Manual, properly applied?

899. How does your organization know that its security arrangements are appropriately effective and constructive?

900. Are people allowed to contribute ideas?

901. How does your organization know whether they

are adhering to mission and achieving objectives?

902. How does your organization know that its staff have appropriate access to a fair and effective grievance process?

903. Is refuse and garbage adequately stored and disposed of with sufficient frequency to prevent contamination?

3.6 Team Directory: MicroStrategy

904. How does the team resolve conflicts and ensure tasks are completed?

905. Who will talk to the customer?

906. Days from the time the issue is identified?

907. Do purchase specifications and configurations match requirements?

908. How will you accomplish and manage the objectives?

909. When will you produce deliverables?

910. What are you going to deliver or accomplish?

911. How will the team handle changes?

912. Process decisions: are all start-up, turn over and close out requirements of the contract satisfied?

913. Process decisions: do invoice amounts match accepted work in place?

914. Process decisions: which organizational elements and which individuals will be assigned management functions?

915. Who will write the meeting minutes and distribute?

916. Timing: when do the effects of communication take place?

917. When does information need to be distributed?

918. Process decisions: how well was task order work performed?

919. Decisions: what could be done better to improve the quality of the constructed product?

920. Who is the Sponsor?

921. Who are your stakeholders (customers, sponsors, end users, team members)?

922. Decisions: is the most suitable form of contract being used?

3.7 Team Operating Agreement: MicroStrategy

923. Did you determine the technology methods that best match the messages to be communicated?

924. Are there more than two functional areas represented by your team?

925. Has the appropriate access to relevant data and analysis capability been granted?

926. What are the current caseload numbers in the unit?

927. What is the anticipated procedure (recruitment, solicitation of volunteers, or assignment) for selecting team members?

928. How will group handle unplanned absences?

929. What resources can be provided for the team in terms of equipment, space, time for training, protected time and space for meetings, and travel allowances?

930. Why does your organization want to participate in teaming?

931. Do you record meetings for the already stated unable to attend?

932. Do you use a parking lot for any items that are

important and outside of the agenda?

933. How will you divide work equitably?

934. What is your unique contribution to your organization?

935. Are there influences outside the team that may affect performance, and if so, have you identified and addressed them?

936. Seconds for members to respond?

937. Do you post any action items, due dates, and responsibilities on the team website?

938. What are the safety issues/risks that need to be addressed and/or that the team needs to consider?

939. What is culture?

940. What individual strengths does each team member bring to the group?

941. How will you resolve conflict efficiently and respectfully?

3.8 Team Performance Assessment: MicroStrategy

942. Which situations call for a more extreme type of adaptiveness in which team members actually re-define roles?

943. What is method variance?

944. To what degree are fresh input and perspectives systematically caught and added (for example, through information and analysis, new members, and senior sponsors)?

945. What makes opportunities more or less obvious?

946. If you have criticized someones work for method variance in your role as reviewer, what was the circumstance?

947. To what degree does the teams approach to its work allow for modification and improvement over time?

948. What are you doing specifically to develop the leaders around you?

949. To what degree is there a sense that only the team can succeed?

950. How does MicroStrategy project termination impact MicroStrategy project team members?

951. How hard did you try to make a good selection?

952. To what degree will the team adopt a concrete, clearly understood, and agreed-upon approach that will result in achievement of the teams goals?

953. To what degree do members understand and articulate the same purpose without relying on ambiguous abstractions?

954. To what degree are staff involved as partners in the improvement process?

955. What are teams?

956. To what degree are the goals realistic?

957. To what degree do team members understand one anothers roles and skills?

958. How hard do you try to make a good selection?

959. Where to from here?

960. Is there a particular method of data analysis that you would recommend as a means of demonstrating that method variance is not of great concern for a given dataset?

961. Social categorization and intergroup behaviour: Does minimal intergroup discrimination make social identity more positive?

3.9 Team Member Performance Assessment: MicroStrategy

962. How are assessments designed, delivered, and otherwise used to maximize training?

963. What are best practices in use for the performance measurement system?

964. How do you know that all team members are learning?

965. Does adaptive training work?

966. Goals met?

967. How do you start collaborating?

968. What evaluation results do you have?

969. Who receives a benchmark visit?

970. What qualities does a successful Team leader possess?

971. What, if any, steps are available for employees who feel they have been unfairly or inaccurately rated?

972. How is assessment information achieved, stored?

973. How often should assessments be conducted?

974. To what degree are the skill areas critical to team performance present?

975. What happens if a team member disagrees with the Job Expectations?

976. What is a significant fact or event?

977. How is your organizations Strategic Management System tied to performance measurement?

978. What are the evaluation strategies (e.g., reaction, learning, behavior, results) used. What evaluation results did you have?

979. What happens if a team member receives a Rating of Unsatisfactory?

980. What are the key duties or tasks of the Ratee?

3.10 Issue Log: MicroStrategy

981. Do you feel more overwhelmed by stakeholders?

982. What is the stakeholders level of authority?

983. Is the issue log kept in a safe place?

984. Who is the stakeholder?

985. What help do you and your team need from the stakeholders?

986. In your work, how much time is spent on stakeholder identification?

987. What effort will a change need?

988. Do you feel a register helps?

989. How do you manage human resources?

990. How is this initiative related to other portfolios, programs, or MicroStrategy projects?

991. How often do you engage with stakeholders?

992. Are there common objectives between the team and the stakeholder?

993. Who have you worked with in past, similar initiatives?

994. What approaches do you use?

995. Are there too many who have an interest in some aspect of your work?

996. Are they needed?

997. Why do you manage human resources?

4.0 Monitoring and Controlling Process Group: MicroStrategy

998. How is agile portfolio management done?

999. What are the goals of the program?

1000. In what way has the program come up with innovative measures for problem-solving?

1001. Is the program making progress in helping to achieve the set results?

1002. Propriety: who needs to be involved in the evaluation to be ethical?

1003. Are the necessary foundations in place to ensure the sustainability of the results of the programme?

1004. Who needs to be engaged upfront to ensure use of results?

1005. How well did the team follow the chosen processes?

1006. Is there sufficient time allotted between the general system design and the detailed system design phases?

1007. What were things that you did very well and want to do the same again on the next MicroStrategy project?

1008. How is agile MicroStrategy project management done?

1009. When will the MicroStrategy project be done?

1010. How should needs be met?

1011. What will you do to minimize the impact should a risk event occur?

1012. Do clients benefit (change) from the services?

1013. How to ensure validity, quality and consistency?

1014. How do you monitor progress?

1015. Accuracy: what design will lead to accurate information?

4.1 Project Performance Report: MicroStrategy

1016. To what degree are the tasks requirements reflected in the flow and storage of information?

1017. To what degree are the demands of the task compatible with and converge with the mission and functions of the formal organization?

1018. To what degree will new and supplemental skills be introduced as the need is recognized?

1019. To what degree can team members frequently and easily communicate with one another?

1020. To what degree are the structures of the formal organization consistent with the behaviors in the informal organization?

1021. To what degree does the information network communicate information relevant to the task?

1022. To what degree is there centralized control of information sharing?

1023. To what degree can the team measure progress against specific goals?

1024. What is the PRS?

1025. To what degree are the goals ambitious?

1026. To what degree can the cognitive capacity of individuals accommodate the flow of information?

1027. To what degree does the teams purpose contain themes that are particularly meaningful and memorable?

1028. To what degree do members articulate the goals beyond the team membership?

1029. What is the degree to which rules govern information exchange between individuals within your organization?

1030. To what degree does the informal organization make use of individual resources and meet individual needs?

4.2 Variance Analysis: MicroStrategy

1031. How does the monthly budget compare to the actual experience?

1032. What causes selling price variance?

1033. What is exceptional?

1034. What is the budgeted cost for work scheduled?

1035. What is the actual cost of work performed?

1036. How are material, labor, and overhead variances calculated and recorded?

1037. Are all elements of indirect expense identified to overhead cost budgets of MicroStrategy projections?

1038. Did an existing competitor change strategy?

1039. There are detailed schedules which support control account and work package start and completion dates/events?

1040. How do you manage changes in the nature of the overhead requirements?

1041. Are the actual costs used for variance analysis reconcilable with data from the accounting system?

1042. Does the contractors system provide unit or lot costs when applicable?

1043. What is the incurrence of actual indirect costs in excess of budgets, by element of expense?

1044. Are the requirements for all items of overhead established by rational, traceable processes?

1045. Are there changes in the direct base to which overhead costs are allocated?

1046. What was the cause of the increase in costs?

1047. Are the bases and rates for allocating costs from each indirect pool consistently applied?

4.3 Earned Value Status: MicroStrategy

1048. Where is evidence-based earned value in your organization reported?

1049. Verification is a process of ensuring that the developed system satisfies the stakeholders agreements and specifications; Are you building the product right? What do you verify?

1050. How does this compare with other MicroStrategy projects?

1051. If earned value management (EVM) is so good in determining the true status of a MicroStrategy project and MicroStrategy project its completion, why is it that hardly any one uses it in information systems related MicroStrategy projects?

1052. Earned value can be used in almost any MicroStrategy project situation and in almost any MicroStrategy project environment. it may be used on large MicroStrategy projects, medium sized MicroStrategy projects, tiny MicroStrategy projects (in cut-down form), complex and simple MicroStrategy projects and in any market sector. some people, of course, know all about earned value, they have used it for years - but perhaps not as effectively as they could have?

1053. How much is it going to cost by the finish?

1054. What is the unit of forecast value?

1055. When is it going to finish?

1056. Where are your problem areas?

1057. Validation is a process of ensuring that the developed system will actually achieve the stakeholders desired outcomes; Are you building the right product? What do you validate?

1058. Are you hitting your MicroStrategy projects targets?

4.4 Risk Audit: MicroStrategy

1059. Do you have a realistic budget and do you present regular financial reports that identify how you are going against that budget?

1060. Extending the consideration on the halo effect, to what extent are auditors able to build skepticism in evidence review?

1061. Who is responsible for what?

1062. Does the implementation method matter?

1063. Is your organization an exempt employer for payroll tax purposes?

1064. Are policies communicated to all affected?

1065. Are procedures in place to ensure the security of staff and information and compliance with privacy legislation if applicable?

1066. How risk averse are you?

1067. What are the outcomes you are looking for?

1068. Does your organization have a social media policy and procedure?

1069. What can you do to manage outcomes?

1070. Are corresponding safety and risk management policies posted for all to see?

1071. Has everyone (staff, volunteers and participants) agreed to a code of behaviour or conduct?

1072. Does your organization have any policies or procedures to guide its decision-making (code of conduct for the board, conflict of interest policy, etc.)?

1073. What is the implication of budget constraint on this process?

1074. Does willful intent modify risk-based auditing?

1075. Is the technology to be built new to your organization?

1076. Is your organization willing to commit significant time to the requirements gathering process?

1077. Is the customer willing to participate in reviews?

4.5 Contractor Status Report: MicroStrategy

1078. What is the average response time for answering a support call?

1079. Who can list a MicroStrategy project as organization experience, your organization or a previous employee of your organization?

1080. How long have you been using the services?

1081. What was the final actual cost?

1082. Describe how often regular updates are made to the proposed solution. Are corresponding regular updates included in the standard maintenance plan?

1083. If applicable; describe your standard schedule for new software version releases. Are new software version releases included in the standard maintenance plan?

1084. What was the budget or estimated cost for your organizations services?

1085. What was the overall budget or estimated cost?

1086. Are there contractual transfer concerns?

1087. How is risk transferred?

1088. What was the actual budget or estimated cost

for your organizations services?

1089. What are the minimum and optimal bandwidth requirements for the proposed solution?

1090. What process manages the contracts?

4.6 Formal Acceptance: MicroStrategy

1091. Was the MicroStrategy project managed well?

1092. Was the sponsor/customer satisfied?

1093. What was done right?

1094. Does it do what client said it would?

1095. Does it do what MicroStrategy project team said it would?

1096. Was the client satisfied with the MicroStrategy project results?

1097. What features, practices, and processes proved to be strengths or weaknesses?

1098. How well did the team follow the methodology?

1099. What lessons were learned about your MicroStrategy project management methodology?

1100. Was the MicroStrategy project goal achieved?

1101. Do you buy pre-configured systems or build your own configuration?

1102. Did the MicroStrategy project achieve its MOV?

1103. How does your team plan to obtain formal acceptance on your MicroStrategy project?

1104. Was the MicroStrategy project work done on time, within budget, and according to specification?

1105. What can you do better next time?

1106. Do you perform formal acceptance or burn-in tests?

1107. Is formal acceptance of the MicroStrategy project product documented and distributed?

1108. Have all comments been addressed?

1109. What are the requirements against which to test, Who will execute?

1110. Who would use it?

5.0 Closing Process Group: MicroStrategy

1111. What is the MicroStrategy project name and date of completion?

1112. What is the risk of failure to your organization?

1113. Does the close educate others to improve performance?

1114. What was learned?

1115. What could have been improved?

1116. What areas does the group agree are the biggest success on the MicroStrategy project?

1117. How will staff learn how to use the deliverables?

1118. When will the MicroStrategy project be done?

1119. Mitigate. what will you do to minimize the impact should a risk event occur?

1120. Were escalated issues resolved promptly?

1121. Did the MicroStrategy project team have enough people to execute the MicroStrategy project plan?

1122. What will you do?

1123. What were the actual outcomes?

1124. Will the MicroStrategy project deliverable(s) replace a current asset or group of assets?

1125. Did the MicroStrategy project team have the right skills?

1126. Were the outcomes different from the already stated planned?

5.1 Procurement Audit: MicroStrategy

1127. Are all checks stored in a secure area?

1128. Do contracts contain regular reviews, targets and quality standards in order to assess suppliers performance?

1129. Are checks disbursed by someone other than the individual who authorized payment?

1130. Were no charges billed to interested economic operators or the parties to the system?

1131. How do you deal with budget constrains and assurance needs?

1132. In case of decisions not to conclude a procurement or award a contract, were tenderers informed in writing and on a timely basis of the already stated decisions and grounds?

1133. Do appropriate controls ensure that procurement decisions are not biased by conflicts of interest or corruption?

1134. Are all complaints of late or incorrect payment sent to a person independent of the already stated having cash disbursement responsibilities?

1135. Relevance of the contract to the Internal Market?

1136. Are risks in the external environment identified,

for example: Budgetary constraints?

1137. Is a risk evaluation performed?

1138. Does the individual approving disbursements sign or initial the document?

1139. In a competitive dialogue, were solutions proposed or confidential information given by a candidate not revealed to others without his/her express agreement?

1140. If an electronic auction or a dynamic purchasing system was used, did the tender documents specify details on access to information, electronic equipment used and connection specifications?

1141. Is there a form specified for bids?

1142. Are outsourcing and Public Private Partnerships considered as alternatives to in-house work?

1143. Are the established budget and timetable (milestones) respected?

1144. Is it clear which procurement procedure your organization has opted for?

1145. Are criteria and sub-criteria set suitable to identify the tender that offers best value for money?

1146. Is there no evidence that the consultants participating in the MicroStrategy project design released information to contractors competing for the prime contract?

5.2 Contract Close-Out: MicroStrategy

1147. What is capture management?

1148. Was the contract complete without requiring numerous changes and revisions?

1149. Have all contracts been completed?

1150. How/when used ?

1151. Change in knowledge?

1152. Change in attitude or behavior?

1153. Why Outsource?

1154. Have all acceptance criteria been met prior to final payment to contractors?

1155. What happens to the recipient of services?

1156. Was the contract sufficiently clear so as not to result in numerous disputes and misunderstandings?

1157. Was the contract type appropriate?

1158. How does it work?

1159. Are the signers the authorized officials?

1160. Have all contracts been closed?

1161. Parties: who is involved?

1162. Change in circumstances?

1163. Have all contract records been included in the MicroStrategy project archives?

1164. Parties: Authorized?

1165. How is the contracting office notified of the automatic contract close-out?

1166. Has each contract been audited to verify acceptance and delivery?

5.3 Project or Phase Close-Out: MicroStrategy

1167. Who is responsible for award close-out?

1168. What advantages do the an individual interview have over a group meeting, and vice-versa?

1169. Did the delivered product meet the specified requirements and goals of the MicroStrategy project?

1170. Is the lesson based on actual MicroStrategy project experience rather than on independent research?

1171. What information did each stakeholder need to contribute to the MicroStrategy projects success?

1172. Were cost budgets met?

1173. What could be done to improve the process?

1174. Complete yes or no?

1175. What can you do better next time, and what specific actions can you take to improve?

1176. What are the marketing communication needs for each stakeholder?

1177. Did the MicroStrategy project management methodology work?

1178. What benefits or impacts does the stakeholder group expect to obtain as a result of the MicroStrategy project?

1179. Which changes might a stakeholder be required to make as a result of the MicroStrategy project?

1180. What process was planned for managing issues/risks?

1181. What stakeholder group needs, expectations, and interests are being met by the MicroStrategy project?

1182. Can the lesson learned be replicated?

1183. What are the informational communication needs for each stakeholder?

1184. Planned completion date?

5.4 Lessons Learned: MicroStrategy

1185. How was the MicroStrategy project controlled?

1186. How well were MicroStrategy project issues communicated throughout your involvement in the MicroStrategy project?

1187. How clearly defined were the objectives for this MicroStrategy project?

1188. What is the supplier dependency?

1189. How effective were MicroStrategy project audits?

1190. Who is responsible for each action?

1191. What are your lessons learned that you will keep in mind for the next MicroStrategy project you participate in?

1192. Which estimation issues did you personally have and what was the impact?

1193. How well prepared were you to receive MicroStrategy project deliverables?

1194. How effectively and timely was your organizational change impact identified and planned for?

1195. Were the MicroStrategy project goals attained?

1196. How much flexibility is there in the funding (e.g., what authorities does the program manager have to change to the specifics of the funding within the overall funding ceiling)?

1197. How timely was the training you received in preparation for the use of the product/service?

1198. Were the aims and objectives achieved?

1199. What is the supervisor to staff ratio?

1200. What is the impact of tax policy?

1201. How adaptable is the deliverable?

1202. What rewards do the individuals seek?

1203. Were quality procedures built into the MicroStrategy project?

1204. How much of your time was spent on other than this MicroStrategy project?

Index

behind 2, 99, 126
belief   12, 17, 25, 35, 51, 69, 79, 87
beliefs 117
believe 2, 109, 136
belong 91
benchmark   245
benefit 3, 20-21, 23, 54, 56, 76, 82, 103, 124, 145, 181, 250
benefits   18, 39, 41, 56, 87, 105, 115, 127, 147, 155, 176, 220, 225, 270
better 9, 31, 39-40, 65, 100, 115, 169, 182, 190, 216, 234, 240, 262, 269
between   43, 53-54, 58, 93, 106, 110, 115, 122, 125, 133, 157, 162, 178, 207, 247, 249, 252
beyond   84, 252
biased 265
bidders   154
bidding   188
biggest   96, 122, 124, 263
billed   265
blackout   125
bottleneck   169
boundaries   32, 53
bounds   32
Breakdown   5, 45, 74, 94, 163, 178
briefed 27
brings 26
broader   118
browser   17
budget   2, 54, 74, 149, 166-167, 182, 184, 192, 253, 257-259, 262, 265-266
Budgetary   266
budgeted   201, 253
Budgeting   43, 54-56, 66, 166
budgets   122, 165-166, 201, 253-254, 269
building   147, 255-256
bullet   128
burden 234
burn-in 262
business   2, 9, 11, 18, 22-23, 25, 27, 29-30, 35-46, 48-49, 51-67, 69-78, 80-81, 83-85, 87-92, 94-101, 103-107, 109-110, 112-113, 115-124, 126-134, 136-137, 143, 145, 155-156, 159, 165, 187, 213, 224-226, 233
businesses   55

278

control 4, 74, 79-80, 83-84, 140, 145-146, 152-153, 160, 165-167, 180, 191, 226-227, 230-231, 234-235, 251, 253
controlled   201, 271
controls   22, 175, 216, 265
converge   251
conversion   53, 122
converted   137
convey   3
cooperate   191
copies 194
Copyright   3
corporate   2, 52, 77, 92, 99, 108, 119
correct35, 79, 102, 135, 184, 186
corrective   82
correctly   105, 112, 131, 147
correspond   10-11
corruption   265
costing165
counting   154
course 32, 255
covering   10, 203
covers 218
crashes   130
crashing   176
create 23, 51, 53, 65, 74, 95, 99, 102, 117, 125, 195
created   144, 149, 181, 205, 210, 222, 227
creating   9, 65, 151
creative   124
creativity   72
credible   191
crimping   128
crisis   23
criteria 4, 6, 10-11, 28, 63, 71, 76, 96-97, 129, 139, 157, 180-181, 190, 192, 220, 266-267
CRITERION   4, 17, 25, 35, 51, 69, 79, 87
critical 28, 31-32, 48, 52, 85, 88, 95, 105, 122, 130, 169, 173-174, 180, 219, 226, 246
criticized   243
crucial 66, 146
crystal 12
cultural76, 118
culture 98, 126, 130, 148, 203, 224, 242

divide 242
Divided   24, 33-34, 49, 67, 78, 86, 138
document   11, 28, 71, 74, 76, 153, 156, 161-162, 205, 221,
234-235, 266
documented 26, 81-83, 107, 140, 168, 192, 202-203, 262
documents   9, 161, 266
domain   42
dominate   101
dossier 46
drawback   222
drawings   237
driven 52-53, 65-66
driving 109
duplicated   129
Duration   5, 163, 180, 182
durations   31, 167, 184
during 32, 52, 78, 98, 130, 141, 177, 189, 200, 214-215, 234
duties   230, 246
dynamic   214, 266
dynamics   29
eagerly   2
earlier 134
earliest 154
earned   7, 200, 255
earnings   53
easily   180, 251
economic   93, 217, 265
economical   152
economy   227
eDiscovery   234-235
edition 10
editor 123
editorial   3
educate   263
educated   1
education   83
effect 122, 211, 257
effective   21, 39-41, 44, 48, 59, 67, 95, 118, 161, 182, 209,
235-238, 271
effects 63, 173, 210, 240
efficiency   38, 44, 64, 70
efficient   97, 111, 121, 148, 229
effort   166-167, 200, 247

refreshed   2
refuse 238
refuses 217
Regarding   91, 96, 108, 111, 123, 130-131, 133, 188, 221, 229
regards   55-56
region 80, 88, 107, 117, 123-124, 128
Register   4, 6, 144, 210, 247
regular 20, 27, 29, 42, 204, 257, 259, 265
regularly   28, 31, 33
regulated   231
regulation   18
regulatory   110, 194
reject 153, 159, 224
rejected   230
rejecting   153
relate 222, 233
related 63, 83, 105, 132, 203, 206, 247, 255
relates 107
relation   36
relational   61
relations   125
release 167, 204, 206
released   266
releases   259
Relevance   265
relevant   28-29, 44, 72, 147, 159, 224, 241, 251
reliable 29, 216
relieved   2
relying 244
remaining   184, 191
remedies   39
remotely   79, 93, 116
remove   76
renewal   53
rephrased   11
replace   264
replanning   165
replicated   43, 47, 270
report 7, 30, 70, 73-74, 85, 90, 94, 96, 99, 101-103, 109, 112, 123,
135, 186, 194, 210, 221, 228, 251, 259
reported   115, 166, 221, 255
reporting   30, 36, 41, 44, 54, 57, 63, 80, 82, 84, 87, 95, 97,
109, 116, 123, 130, 132, 151, 165, 194, 201

reports 2, 38, 43, 45, 54, 58, 61, 63, 92, 94, 100, 114, 131, 144,
187, 208, 218, 222, 257
repository   66
represent   193, 232
represents   128
reproduced   3
reputation   125
request   7, 192-193, 230-233
requested   3, 130, 220, 230, 232
requests   67, 124, 230
require 71, 125, 166, 177, 184, 211-212
required   29, 32, 34, 62, 65, 92, 141, 145, 151, 162, 169-171,
182, 198, 206, 210, 212, 214, 222, 224, 237, 270
requires   221
requiring   144, 267
research   39, 113, 269
reserved   3
reside   132, 221
residual   166
resolution   134
resolve 23, 119, 239, 242
resolved   184, 208, 263
Resource   5-6, 61, 167, 177-178, 204, 222, 227-228
resources   2, 4, 9, 29, 46, 52, 74, 93, 97, 106, 113, 142, 145,
154-155, 169, 171, 178, 183, 186, 190, 192, 219, 222, 241, 247-248,
252
respect   3
respected   266
respond   18, 14/-148, 210, 242
responded   13
responding   210
response   23, 81-82, 85, 209, 220, 259
responses   135, 211, 221
responsive   191
restating   108
result   53, 190, 197, 207, 232, 244, 267, 270
resulted   83
resulting   56, 165
results 10, 19-21, 31-32, 36, 41, 53, 66, 69, 82, 119, 127, 147-148,
190, 198, 221, 226, 245-246, 249, 261
retain   87, 117
retained   113
retention   47, 112

Made in the USA
Las Vegas, NV
29 September 2022

56197646R00185